Dr. CASS INGRAM

The Wild Turmeric Cure

KNOWLEDGE
HOUSE
PUBLISHERS

Printed in the United States of America

ISBN: 9781931078432

Disclaimer: This book is not intended as a substitute for medical diagnosis or treatment. Anyone who has a serious disease should consult a physician before initiating any change in treatment or before beginning any new treatment.

To order this or additional Knowledge House books call: 1-800-295-3737 or order via the web at: www.cassingram.com

For a brochure and order form send a SASE with three
US first class stamps to:
Knowledge House Publishers
105 East Townline Rd., Unit 116
Vernon Hills, IL 60061

Table of Contents

Introduction

What is *The Wild Turmeric Cure*? It is a revelation of the true miracle powers of nature, known to ancient societies but rarely understood by modern humans. The word 'wild' is a part of this title, since this book describes a special type of turmeric. It's the wild-growing type, which is not raised, industrially, on farms. Yet, even so, farm-raised turmeric, if managed without the use of synthetic chemicals and fertilizers, if free of all contaminants, is also an invaluable medicine. In this regard certified organic is superior to commercial grades. Even so, beyond all these is wild turmeric, which has a higher density of active ingredients than even organic and, thus, greater medicinal power than all others.

Turmeric is both a miracle and a cure. Why is it a miracle? This is because of the fact that this natural cure is available to all, even though it has been, until recently, largely overlooked and neglected. Who hasn't consumed turmeric in its many common forms: in curry powder, as an individual spice added to recipes, or as that coloring of tandoori meat or as a coloring in Indian and African rice dishes? Others have consumed it as a main ingredient of pickled mangos, still others as a dye in mustard. However, despite decades of use and consumption virtually no one considered it a medicinal herb, one that could be taken for the prevention and reversal of major degenerative diseases.

Yet, the plethora of research demonstrates that turmeric is a potent, invaluable natural medicine, even though in most people's minds it is nothing other than a lowly spice, perhaps at best a food coloring.

All spices are powerful medicines, virtually drug-like. Cinnamon controls blood sugar as well as any drug, while cloves kill pain almost as well as anesthetics. Wild oregano is a more powerful germ killer than any antibiotic. Rosemary is a more effective antidepressant than mood altering drugs. Thus, the reason for the spice wars of prior civilizations can now be known. Regarding turmeric, it was held as invaluable, because of its ability to keep food fresh and germ-free longer: without refrigeration. Because of its preservative properties at one time it played such a vital role in South Asia that it was held more valuable than gold and precious stones. Entire nations fought each other to control spices. It couldn't have been only because of their culinary value. In fact, they are invaluable as natural drugs, as well as food preservatives, and the rulers and other powerful ones of the past realized this. Moreover, unlike modern-day drugs spices are completely edible, so they can be used with impunity. They can not only be added to food as desired but are also powerful in the treatment and prevention of disease.

The powers of turmeric alone are extremely diverse. It is so utilitarian that no drug can compare. This is because of its novel mechanism of action. Drugs are produced to affect only single elements, known biochemically as a signaling pathway. It is the genes which control such a biochemical course through a mechanism known as gene expression. In contrast, turmeric impacts multiple signaling pathways simultaneously. Thus, it directly and systematically influences a plethora of genes. This means it is far more 'intelligent' than any of the so-called smart drugs the pharmaceutical companies can produce. It also means it is more effective: incomparably so.

Only the Divine Source in His magnificence could be responsible for such a phenomenon. This Being created such a sophisticated complex, which is so universal in its powers, that it can be used for the reversal of dozens of diseases. Thus, there is now hope for the effective treatment of disease syndromes that had previously been deemed incurable. In this regard it is important to give thanks, just like, for instance, the aboriginal people have done to nature as well as the High Spirit. These aborigines even bless the earth, as well as individual herbs or plants, for their benefits. Thanking the medicine, and, particularly, the merciful Force behind it, that is being grateful, aids in the power of the cure.

Now, here is a most curious element. Every attempt to improve upon or match this creator's handiwork has failed. For instance, isolates of turmeric are far less effective in therapeutic powers than whole plant extracts. Even the whole spice, either as the fresh root or a high-grade food powder, if used correctly, is medicinal. Moreover, attempts have been made to synthesize the presumed active ingredient, in this case a compound known as curcumin. However, the artificial production has proven relatively impotent compared to the wholly natural type and has also caused significant side-effects. Despite this, the pharmaceutical industry is making every effort to popularize such artificial components.

Furthermore, there is the issue of corrupting the whole. There are major consequences from chemical treatment and isolation of turmeric active ingredients. As will be demonstrated, here, the use of harsh solvents, which include chlorinated hydrocarbons and gasoline-like molecules, do not enhance the end result. Though they do act to isolate and concentrate active ingredients these solvents weaken the turmeric, depleting its effectiveness.

People are interested in turmeric; it is becoming an international phenomenon. There are now dozens of supplements available, all touting that they have the advantage over the others: that they are the best, most well absorbed, and/or most potent. What is a person to do to in order to make a sound decision on which supplement to use? How does the individual navigate all this? This book will act to clarify any such confusion. It will describe precisely the forms of turmeric that are most health-giving and which ones are, in contrast, relatively impotent. One simple element in this regard is to follow the ways of nature. Without human meddling turmeric stands on its own as a natural medicinal complex with over 100 active ingredients. Following nature means using turmeric in crude, whole food forms such as the wild and organic spice powder, the whole, naturally grown root, and any supplements, which are whole food-based.

Yet, how could any turmeric extract, commercial or otherwise, be impotent? Through chemical processing it is possible to alter powerful, natural drugs to the point that their efficacy is limited. Here, the emphasis is on the least processed forms of turmeric. It is these types which most effectively reverse and prevent a wide range of diseases. Such types are also the most ideal for daily/long-term use. Incredibly, such whole food forms are the most reliable for producing measurable results, despite the hype behind popular turmeric/curcumin supplements.

Too, it is best to use a combination of these biological complexes in order to achieve the most thorough results. They all have their advantages and in some cases, disadvantages. For instance, with the food powder extensive heat is applied, which leads to the loss of delicate compounds, notably the essential oils, although the rest of the complex remains intact. Regarding the raw root, while it contains all the turmeric active ingredients, optimal absorption is an issue. In the typical supplements, usually, great amounts of heat are applied, which may lead to the loss of active ingredients. In others, the heating is kept to a minimum, for instance, through the use of alcohol and/or CO_2 extraction.

So, it is information gathering that leads to sound choices. This makes the journey more enjoyable. For instance, it will be found, here, that the food forms are reasonable choices and in some instances are just as effective as many supplements. Whole food forms can be consumed in a variety of recipes, novel beverages, and smoothies. Likewise, there is a place for supplements, and the efficacy, along with potency, of these varies greatly. As well, there are issues of optimal absorption in all cases: food forms and supplemental. Furthermore, whole food supplements are just as described, food. Thus, they can be taken with impunity in as large of quanity as is both desired and needed. Since they are food additives this means that the individual can gain the benefits while entirely relishing in the process with great taste and gusto.

What is turmeric?

Turmeric is a root or, more correctly, a rhizome of the ginger family. For thousands of years it has been used as a medicine and also as a nutritious food, along with a cosmetic. As a spice it is a standard in Indian, Pakistani, Asian, and North African cuisine and is much used also in Middle Eastern cookery. As a dye it is used in textiles and also to color food. For instance, in South Africa and Persia it is traditional to add it to rice, giving it a yellow color.

What is it used for?

Traditionally, turmeric has been used for the treatment of certain diseases and/or conditions. The main therapeutic applications are as follows:

- as an antiseptic for cuts, burns, scrapes, and bruises
- as a generalized antibacterial agent
- for purifying the blood
- for reversing chronic skin conditions, including eczema and psoriasis
- as an antiinflammatory agent
- for relief of minor to moderate gastrointestinal disorders, including irritable bowl syndrome
- for improving overall digestion
- for expelling worms
- for regulating menstruation
- for dissolution of gallstones and for aiding liver function
- for relieving the pain and inflammation of arthritis

The above list would be the uses adopted by common people. According to S. Prasad and B.B. Aggarwal in their summary chapter, "Turmeric, the Gold Spice" there are also a number of other historical uses by traditional Indian practitioners, known as Ayurvedic doctors, the suffix 'vedic' arising from the spiritual scriptures, the vedas. These traditional uses are as follows:

- for easing and relieving asthma and for expelling mucous plugs
- for overall toning of the liver and reversal of hepatic disorders, like jaundice and hepatitis
- for relieving rheumatic pains
- topically for healing diabetic ulcers
- in the treatment of sinusitis
- for causing increased drainage from the sinuses
- topically on sprains and other traumatic injuries
- for eye disorders such as conjunctivitis and cataract
- to ease abdominal pain and bloating

What is it made of?

This is, perhaps, the most important question of all. Turmeric consists of some 100-plus components, all of which are medicinal and/or nutritious. By weight the main component is the volatile oils. As a group these volatile substances are represented by the turmerones and also the pigments, known as curcuminoids. The curcuminoids are held by many as the most important of all active ingredients, although this is now under dispute. This group is represented by three compounds:

- curcumin, that is demethoxycurcumin
- 5-methoxycurcumin
- dihydrocurcumin

These substances largely account for the brilliant yellow color of this spice. The other major colorants are the turmerones. The curcumin compounds, along with the turmerones, amount to some 4% to 8% of the total weight. The remaining volatile oils add up to about 3.5% and consist of dozens of substances. Next, there are the plant sterols, including plant cholesterol and beta sitosterol, along with newly discovered novel compounds, known as turmeric polysaccharides. There is a considerable amount of mineral matter in this root, mainly iron but also potassium, phosphorus, and sodium. Regarding vitamins, ascorbic acid, niacin, and riboflavin are found in good amounts. Turmeric is also a good source of omega 3 fatty acids, especially the rather rare alpha linolenic acid, the latter being necessary for the health of all cell membranes.

Chapter One

Turmeric: the Basics

The basic issue regarding this spice is the fact that the whole food form is the most medicinal, just like its cousin, ginger. Here is the key point. It should be treated like a food, not as a drug to be manipulated and isolated. The studies are clear. It is the full complement of this spice's components that accounts for its broad-spectrum, medicinal actions, not merely one or two isolated elements.

The curcumin issue and more

There are essentially two kinds of turmeric, the cultivated types and the various wild species. The cultivated ones are known as *Curcuma longa, although many wild derivatives also carry this same name. In fact, there is not a great deal of difference, botanically, between the two.* Between the wild species and the domesticated ones there are some 50 varieties of this spice. All are members of the ginger family and have much in common with that plant. Prominent authors, such as A. Bagchi of West Bengal University of Technology note that curcumin is the most "active" component, although according to other investigators the essential oils are even more potent. Even so, curcumin is a novel compound. Bagchi has described that there are three forms of this molecule alone, curcumin I, II, and III, listed previously by their chemical names. It is represented, upon extraction, by a yellow, crystalline powder that cannot be dissolved in water and can only be solubilized in fat, including fat-dissolving solvents. This means curcumin is insoluble in water. The absorption of all curcumin isolates is a major challenge, a subject that will be covered thoroughly in this book.

Molecular nature

Why is turmeric so diverse in its powers? This is a consequence of its complex molecular nature. As is obvious from its appearance it is largely a pigment-based natural medicine, although the spice also contains a rich content of essential oils. The pigments appear to be among the most potent compounds and include the most well-studied one, curcumin, which is largely responsible for the spice's deep yellowish-orange color. Curcumin itself is a highly aggressive antioxidant and antiinflammatory agent, because of its specific structure as a polyphenol. It is known, biochemically, as a "highly pleiotropic molecule," which means it is exceedingly diverse. Essentially, it denotes a multiplicity of actions simultaneously. It is also known, chemically, as a polyphenolic phytochemical of the specialized diketone family. In nature the specific types of phytochemicals seen in turmeric, such as its diketone pigments, are relatively rare.

There are yet additional rare substances in turmeric, primarily the essential oils known as tumerones, many of which are unique to the plant. Other novel essential oils found in turmeric are curidone and curzenone-C. There are also more commonly occurring essential oil elements such as eugenol, the active ingredient of cloves, along with cineole, pinene, terpineol, and borneol. All such compounds work in unison to create this medicine's wide-ranging effects. Regardless, there could be no more invaluable mechanism of action than this biological diversity, and this, in fact, is the nature of countless other natural cures. Because of this vast complexity and chemical novelty taking turmeric and/or its extracts means that, at once, the person gains the following benefits:

- anti-pain actions
- antiinflammatory effect
- balancing and lowering of blood sugar (anti-diabetic action)
- antioxidant effect
- wound healing capacity
- anti-histaminic or anti-allergy actions
- anti-tumor actions
- antidote or anti-toxic actions
- anti-degenerative capacities, in particular in relation to brain cells
- regenerative powers for nerve cells as well as endocrine and immunological organs

Is this not a most phenomenal power? Even so, it is not possible to achieve such wide ranging benefits from petro-chemically treated and artificially produced turmeric supplements. This diversity applies to truly whole food turmeric supplements, as well as the naturally/organically grown spice itself, because it is this vast range of capacity, this wholeness and fullness, that accounts for these immense benefits. Chemical isolates and highly refined supplements simply cannot compare in therapeutic powers. Yet, despite this, every effort is being made to produce turmeric synthetically, that is to produce an isolated active ingredient, selling it as a chemical drug.

This is a most erroneous approach. This whole food root represents a live, vital force. In fact, it is filled with energy from the sun and earth, and, thus, it has its own special healing properties, which are unique. By no means can it be duplicated in a sterile lab. Consider its basic ingredients: resins, pigments, volatile oils, albumen, lignins, biological salts, bio-active minerals, and plant sterols. In synthetic versions none of these are included. Nor as a group are they found in the concentrated isolates. Furthermore, it is particularly high in manganese, magnesium, silicon, and iron, none of which are found in highly processed supplements or patented drugs. Then, too, there are lesser components, for instance, vitamin A, as beta carotene, thiamin, vitamin E, riboflavin, boron, sodium, niacin, potassium, selenium, and zinc. Additionally, it is dense in fat, which aids in the absorption of the active components. Can such a broad-spectrum complex really be improved upon through, for instance, the application of harsh extraction processes or via laboratory synthesis?

It is even more profound, if not sophisticated, than this. In his book *Essential Herbs* James Duke, Ph.D., lists the ultimate sources of turmeric's medicinal power as arising from the sophistication of the whole through a list of novel phytochemical compounds in a most outstanding array. The following complete list is found on the Duke database, slightly modified:

- COX-2 inhibitors, notably curcumin
- cineole, a nervous system stimulant and antiseptic
- alpha and beta pinene, essential oil components
- alpha atlantone
- 4-hydroxy-methyl-anthraquinone
- alpha terpineol
- ar-tumerone
- arabinose
- azulene
- beta sesquiphellandrene
- bisdesmethoxycurcumin
- bisabolene
- borneol
- caffeic acid
- caprylic acid
- caryophyllene, an essential oil component
- cinnamic acid
- curcumene, an essential oil component found in large amounts
- curcumenol, an essential oil component
- curcumin, an antioxidant pigment found in large amounts
- dihydrocurcumin
- desmethoxycurcumin
- diferuloylmethane
- guaiacol
- zingiberene
- vanillic acid
- tumerone, found in relatively large amounts
- curdione, an antitumor substance
- curlone
- curzerenone
- cyclo-isoprenemyrcene, a root element found in large

amounts
- d-alpha-phellandrene
- d-camphene
- d-camphor
- d-sabinene
- dehydroturmerone
- dicinnamoylmethane
- p-methoxycinnamic acid
- p-cymene
- eugeono, essential oil component
- terpineol, an essential oil component
- terpinene, an essential oil component
- miscellaneous fixed oils, including hormone-like plant sterols

Source with modification: Dr. James Duke, Phytochemical Database, USDA, Beltsville Agricultural Research Center, Beltsville, MD.

Count them. If the vitamins and minerals are added, there are well over 70 compounds. This does not include the protein content, which is considerable. This makes it clear that isolation of single active ingredients is a faulty approach. Through this the miraculous nature of turmeric's curative powers, that refined benefit of its wide-ranging effects, will be lost. If a supplement is to be taken, it must be as wholesome as possible, containing as many of the naturally occuring components as possible.

The beginning

The origin of use for any natural medicine is where all investigation must begin, and the same holds true of turmeric. Traditional methods include mashing/grinding it in a mortar to make a paste. This is then mixed with other spices for flavoring curries. It is also occasionally eaten raw and also chopped and put in salads. Today, however, the most common usage is as a powder. It is prepared in a way it could be preserved: by boiling the root, then drying the root matter, then pulverizing the dry material into a powder. This was both for food and medicinal use.

The main use of the locals, particularly those of Indian culture, was for inflammatory conditions. In Chinese medicine it was relied upon for digestive disorders, including liver and gallbladder conditions. In this regard it is well known that turmeric increases the flow of bile. The Chinese also utilized it for menstrual excess or lack, as a detoxification or internal cleansing agent, as a tonic agent for the intestines and for reducing bleeding disorders, like nose bleeds, hematemesis, excess menstrual bleeding, hemorrhoids, and hematuria. Regarding the latter it proved reliable for normalizing any such bleeding disorders.

It was not just the Chinese and the Hindus, who popularized this. The genus name itself, curcuma, derives from the Arabic, "kurkum," indicating probable use in drug therapy during the Islamic Empire and, certainly, Moghul India. That name indicates that the West received its first introduction through the translation of Islamic texts.

The most well-documented use was in Ayurvedic India, where it held such greatness, historically, that it was given some 50 different names. For Ayurvedic doctors it was used in the fresh root form, a freshly squeezed root juice, in a boiled tea, as an alcohol tincture, in powder form, as a cream or lotion, and boiled in milk and sugar. For sprains a paste was applied combined with lime and salt. It was even burnt, with the fumes being inhaled for lung disorders and liver conditions. Topically, it was applied to hemorrhoids in a base of mustard oil and/or flaxseed oil. It was also used topically for shingles, chickenpox, ulcerations, and blemishes. Yet, it was not merely the Ayurvedic-inclined Indians who relied upon it. The ancient Hawaiians also utilized it, in particular, for sinus infections as well as earaches. An extract was put directly in the sinuses and ears for this purpose. They also found it effective for stomach and intestinal ulcers.

Modern investigations

It seems incredible that it was so neglected, since it is such a crucial medicinal complex, in fact, perhaps the most important one in the Ayurvedic system, being incorporated into countless formulas and drugs. Western herbalists simply did not understand turmeric, at least not until the late 20th century. Then, as a result of impressive scientific findings modern herbalists have become enlightened. This was in part stimulated by the pharmaceutical industry, which began researching the spice intensively. This was largely motivated by a human clinical study, where an extract of turmeric was found highly effective in reversing, in fact, curing gallbladder disorders, notably inflammation of the organ, known as cholecystitis.

The history of turmeric is fascinating, some of which has been alluded to. Yet, it behooves the investigative mind to pursue this in greater detail. It was 20th century research that revolutionized the spice's status. The initial work was done in Germany, where in the early 1920s some of the key active ingredients of the essential oil, the sesquiterpenes, were isolated and determined to have therapeutic activity. Later, a team of scientists compared the effects of whole extract, the essential oil plus the water-soluble extract. By 1936 the yellow dye component, curcumin, had been isolated. This was another key active ingredient, which was then compared to the whole extract. It was found that turmeric and/or its components have definitive actions upon the body, acting in the following ways:

- stimulation of the flow of bile
- increasing the contraction power of the gallbladder wall

This caused a degree of enthusiasm over the root, leading to countless scientific studies over the decades.

While Western laboratories confirmed its powers in Asia researchers were independently validating its properties. The focus, here, was on the hepatoprotective actions, where turmeric was found to block liver toxicity from a wide range of assaults. People use milk thistle for this, but turmeric was found equally effective. Other investigators found it to prevent excessive cholesterol levels in the blood following heavy meals. In the essential oil of turmeric powerful antiinflammatory substances were discovered. In this action it was found to work on an adrenal gland mechanism, indicating it helps modulate and/or conserve cortisol. This is because in experimental studies if the adrenals are removed, the antiinflammatory action of turmeric is lost.

Ultimately, it was recognized but not to a major degree. It was R. Weiss's in *Herbal Medicine*, 1961, who initiated a degree of popularization, where he deemed the spice to be effective as a "gallbladder remedy" through its ability to powerfully induce the production and release of bile, this, of course, based on the German findings. In this regard reports show that in India and other Asian countries it has a long tradition for the treatment of jaundice and various liver diseases. Weiss adds, "There is no doubt that it can be effective, particularly where bile flow needs to be thoroughly stimulated…." Yet, the author then diminished this, stating that, somehow, turmeric would cause 'hyperacidity' and 'gastric irritation,' though not providing any substance to support this, then calling caution for its intake. This derogatory attitude was mere medical arrogance make no mistake. By the 1980s it was recommended by orthodox herbalists for liver detoxification and menstrual regulation. In the 1990s prominent men in the herbal medicine world began touting it, including M. Castelman, David Mowrey, and Michael Tierra, touting it a powerful agent for reversing a number of diseases.

Getting the terminology straight

Turmeric is the name of the whole spice, the standard type belonging to the genus/species, *Curcuma longa*. Like ginger, it is a rhizome or root component. With a tough outer skin, internally, this rhizome is a deep orange color. The orange-yellow color is derived from chemicals known as curcuminoids and also turmerones. The most well known of these is curcumin. As mentioned previously it is associated with related compounds, at least two others with similar properties, that is demetoxycurcumin and bisdemethoxycurcumin. The combination of these compounds is known as curcuminoids. The value, therapeutically, of turmeric and/or its extracts is measured by total curcumionid content, although this is misleading. This is because there are a number of other key active ingredients, for instance, the turmerones, which are in many ways equally as powerful as this complex.

It's a mistake to focus on the main-content element, curcumin alone. As is common in nature there is a grand interaction of all the elements, a synergy within all the key components. In fact, as demonstrated by Jacob in *PPAR Research* the other curcuminoid components of lesser percentage that are often neglected and minimized, like demetoxycurcumin, are just "as effective as pure (in fact, purified) curcumin."

Consider, too, the tumerones. These are aromatic compounds; actually, they are tumeric-based essential oils. In fact, these compounds occur in even a higher density than curcumin. Tumerones are destroyed by most extraction processes. Yet, they are among the most potent turmeric-based substances of all, in many respects more potent than curcumin itself. Thus, let us review the most well understood turmeric active principles in order to understand the medicinal potential of this blessed spice.

Curcumin simply explained

The polyphenol curcumin is the major yellow pigment in turmeric. It is the main compound advertised in turmeric-based dietary supplements, where it is held as the ultimate active ingredient, in particular, for fighting inflammation. As a rule the curcuminoid complex is poorly absorbed. Absorption can be enhanced by the simultaneous intake of certain spices, notably ginger, black pepper, wild oregano, and rosemary. It is also enhanced by the intake of fat such as the fat of meat, milk, and heavy vegetable oils, for instance, oils of black seed, mustard, sesame, or olive. As well, the fats of nut milks, whole, natural milk, and the fatty compounds of coconut aid absorption and assimilation. Traditionally, then, turmeric is used with mustard oil, as in curried mangoes, for a sound purpose, as such oil renders it more soluble.

As will be demonstrated, here, the main power of this pigment relates to its antiinflammatory actions, although there is good data demonstrating its capacity to improve the function of the heart, liver, gallbladder, and brain. It also helps protect the skin from oxidative damage, while exerting significant anticancer properties for virtually all organs of the body.

The biochemistry of curcumin, in particular, is well established. Its beneficial effects are largely mediated by its capacity to facilitate the upregulation of receptor sites involved with inflammation and/or cell overgrowth. The main receptor site influenced by this substance is proliferator-activated receptor, or PPAR. Effectively, curcumin blocks its activation. In this regard it acts as an "extraordinarily potent hydrogen atom donor," a mechanism responsible for extensive oxygen scavenging capacity. Moreover, ascorbic acid and vitamin E, among other antioxidants, like rosemary and oregano, prevent the degradation of curcumin, therefore extending its antioxidant powers. It is the antioxidant properties of turmeric, that is its ability to block free radical-induced cellular degeneration, that largely accounts for its therapeutic powers. This is why the addition of wild oregano and rosemary is so invaluable.

Turmerones

The turmerones are, as mentioned, components of turmeric essential oils. It makes sense that the essential oils are a crucial component. They amount to up to 9% of the total weight, some two to three times more than curcumin content. The turmerone-based essential oils are as follows:

- alpha-curcumene
- beta-curcumene
- zingeberene
- beta sesuiphellandrine
- beta allantone
- germacrone

Highly biologically active, the turmerones have a particularly novel power in regard to the nervous system. They are also exceedingly powerful as anticancer agents, among a host of other functions. Scientific studies demonstrate incredibly powerful actions of these essential oil components. Consider the work of A. Murakami in *Biofactors*. Here, it was found that the tumerones are so powerful that they "abolish tumor formation." This was thought to be due to their ability to suppress nitric oxide formation in macrophages. These substances also suppressed the gene-induced formation of inflammatory compounds. In the study when provocateurs of tumor formation were used to create artificial cancers the tumerones suppressed this, blocking tumor formation more successfully than curcumin alone. Yet another conclusion of this work is the fact that these essential oils suppress inflammation within the colon walls, a major therapeutic benefit.

In another investigation Japanese investigators evaluated the compounds versus human leukemia cells. Incredibly, the turmerones selectively induced the death of the leukemia cell lines. Cancer DNA was broken to smithereens by the turmeric oil molecules, proving that leukemia is vulnerable to this spice oil component. In breast cancer, too, turmerone was found effective, blocking pro-cancer enzyme activators.

Additionally, cancer activators were unable to bind to cells as a result of the turmeric therapy, while COX-2 enzyme promoters were significantly blocked. The growth and invasion by breast cancer cells was significantly inhibited and reversed by turmerone. Korean investigators at Dongseo University, 2009, determined its power against yet another highly destructive cancer, lymphoma. Turmerone essential oil vigorously induced lymphoma cell death through apoptosis.

The turmerones are also highly biologically active within the nervous system. These volatile oils readily cross the blood-brain barrier, where they act positively on the nerve centers. Here, they have been found to activate not only existing neurons but also the stem cells, those responsible for regenerating the brain.

Chapter Two

Extraction and Absorption

Without the use of solvents it is well established that the curcuminoids are almost impossible to extract from turmeric. The standard method for extraction is the so-called Soxhlet method. This involves an extensive process, including a heating time of up to 12 hours. The method is based upon the chemical nature of curcuminoids as being largely insoluble. In order to remove them these pigments are essentially soaked thoroughly in powerful solvents. The solvents used must be driven off with heat for a number of hours, as mentioned. The excessive use of heat and solvents causes the loss of certain delicate active ingredients, particularly the terpenes and essential oils.

Such an intensive procedure is seemingly necessary, because of the nature of the active ingredients. Curcumin and its associated molecules are largely trapped in oleoresin cells. These cells are surrounded by tightly packed cells, known as cork cells, resulting in the need to soak the turmeric for prolonged periods in the solvents. Here, it should be kept in mind that pigments, in general, are notoriously difficult to extract from plants.

A more modernized, standard extraction procedure is described by Kudkarni and his group of the Department of

Biotechnology, Sinhgad College of Engineering, Pune, India. The turmeric is sliced and sun-dried for a week. Then, it is dried again at 50 degrees Centigrade in a hot oven for up to six hours. By a mill it is then powdered.

At this point it is added to the solvent extraction apparatus. The solvent is heated and, then, the turmeric powder is added. In this study selected solvents included chloroform, ethyl acetate, acetone, and methanol. Once it is extracted, as mentioned, the solvents are driven off. The remaining element is a powder, usually reddish brown or blackish-red in color. The highly poisonous methanol yielded the highest level of curcuminoids.

Solvent extraction, another review

Another method is a 12 hour alcohol soak, combined with agitation at a speed of 30 rpm, the drug to solvent ratio of one part drug to six parts ethanol. The strength of the alcohol is usually 70% proof. In certain cases, for instance, in the making of Turmeric-PLUS, the alcohol used is certified organic and no other chemicals are applied.

Still another is the following: to take the dried turmeric rhizomes and subject them to "solvent extraction." This requires the raw material to be turned into a coarse powder and then pelletized. At this point acetone, that is 'fingernail polish fluid,' and/or ethyl acetate is used to repeatedly "wash" the raw material, which selectively extracts the yellow pigment.

The next process is distillation, which drives out the solvent, yielding a liquid matter with a reddish-brown color. This liquid resin is treated with yet another solvent, isopropyl alcohol or rubbing alcohol. The purpose of this step is to extract out the naturally occurring resins, which, by the way, are necessary for optimal absorption. Those resins, now being lost, the process yields a powdered, purified product. This is known as curcumin powder, which is up to 95% 'pure.' This is the process used to make the patented product, Curcumin C3 Complex made by Sabinsa. Obviously, as a result of such processing there is severe damage inflicted on the medicinal molecules.

The use of industrial chemicals, though, such as acetone, ethyl acetate, and isopropyl alcohol, is less than ideal. No herb or spice can be subjected to such extreme degrees of treatment without alteration of active ingredients. As well, it makes no sense to isolate only one substance at the expense of all others. It is the balance of all the natural, God-given chemicals that make turmeric so unique. Regardless, compared to any extract subjected to petrochemical solvents a person would be better off to consume wild or organic turmeric powder or, perhaps, a supplement extracted with alcohol or supercritical carbon, these latter methods being the least noxious in regard to damaging the delicate spice complex.

In this regard it should be kept in mind that alcohol is not as harsh as the petrochemical agents. Thus, there is value in alcoholic extraction, particularly in dissolving and rendering available the tough to extract curcuminoids. People drink alcohol, but no one in their right mind would consume acetone, isopropyl alcohol, or ethyl acetate, which can be fatal upon ingestion and, thus, require treatment from a poison control center.

Think about it. Who would do so normally? Who would consume, for instance, fresh turmeric or the dried shaker spice if realizing it had been soaked in lighter fluid-like or fingernail polish-like substances? The fact is no one would knowingly do so. This is why, here, only the whole food and/or minimally processed sources are recommended. Additionally, in many cases regarding the solvent residues these are disease-causing. Once again, the exceptions are ethanol extracts, which have no significant residual toxicity, particularly if the alcohol source is non-GMO and/or organic.

Now, this is an important revelation. It means that all curcumin/turmeric supplements touting to be 70% or more curcumin are solvent extracted. It also means they undergo similar processes, all of it chemical. No wonder people are getting equivocal results with such supplements as well as the fact that the study results are not entirely compelling. To get the real power from this spice, to garner the multiplicity of its benefits, it is necessary to consume it in the whole, unprocessed form, whether supplementally or in food. This is how the ancients did it, and this is how it should be done today.

This requires some defining. It can be highly confusing when evaluating turmeric supplements. It is easy, though, to determine which ones have been extensively processed. Any supplement touting to have "pure" curcumin is solvent extracted and, thus, heavily processed. The term "purified" also indicates extreme degrees of processing.

Purification is a misnomer. The correct description is chemical extraction for purposes of creating isolates and concentrates. This is through the use of powerful petrochemical solvents and/or chemical-grade alcohol to isolate the desired components at the expense of all other key elements. Purification really means the purging of countless naturally occurring substances in the target plant. Thus, when that term is seen, it should be replaced in the thought process with "isolate" or "isolation." The isolation process is also known as "standardization." This merely means that a standardized amount of the desired component is found in the end product. It's a marketing issue, not a medicinal one.

Think about it. What good would broccoli be if only one chemical was 'isolated' for human use, while all others were discarded, as if they have no value at all? What about carrots? Is it merely the carotene that is health-giving in these roots? Everyone knows that it is the multiplicity of naturally occurring substances that makes these vegetables healthy, not only one or two known ingredients.

Thus, it is seen on the labels, for instance, "standardized to 95% curcuminoids..." or in order to supercede such claims in one case "pure curcuminoids, 97% pure." Still another major player claims to be "95% micronized *Curcuma longa.*" Other label claims include 25 to 1 extract with 95% total curcuminoids and "surface-controlled particle dispersion of turmeric root," None of these sound natural or whole food-based even to the slightest degree.

How anyone could use the terms "pure" and/or "purified" to describe solvent extracted botanicals is hard to fathom, unless it is meant to describe the absolute purging and cleansing from the final solution all the other crucial active ingredients. This purging, though, is most destructive. All the plant ingredients work in an intelligent synergy, and no one understands the complete mechanism. It is arrogant beyond belief for people to hold that one or more isolated ingredients is responsible for the ultimate medicinal action. The standardization process amounts to the fragmentation of nature, where the mysterious powers of the whole are entirely neutralized. Dozens of complex compounds are lost at the expense of one or two active ingredients. These compounds include terpenes, essential oils, naturally occurring long chain alcohols, resins, waxes, and sterols. All such components are essential for maximizing the spice's medicinal actions. Maximizing the dose of only a few purported active ingredients cannot match the synergy of the whole.

The bioavailability issue

Absorption and bioavailability are similar. Yet, there has been much discussion about how well turmeric or its components can be absorbed into the bloodstream. There is sound reason for this. Regarding the pigments, in particular, a number of studies have found poor absorption, that is low or even negligent blood levels, after administration. Yet, these studies were done on the isolate, curcumin, which is as a rule exceedingly difficult to absorb. The whole turmeric complex is much more readily processed and absorbed than standardized supplements. In fact, by adding other tumeric components to curcumin, like turmeric essential oil, curcumin bioavailability is greatly enhanced.

This makes sense. Each plant is a synergistic complex. Only the almighty creator knows best the ultimate nature of any such complex. It's human short-sightedness to hold only a single component of many as the key. Consider that litany of other crucial components: turmerin, turmerone, furanodiene, germacrone, elemene, curidione, and cyclocurcumin. Clearly, then, the whole complex turmeric is far more powerful and effective than isolated, manipulated versions. The co-factors are there for a reason. For optimal benefits always consume the whole complex, whether in the food form, as turmeric powder, or as a truly unprocessed whole food supplement. This is particularly true to gain the wide-ranging benefits of this spice on all the body systems.

It's now known that turmeric and its components are highly medicinal, although the majority of research has focused on curcumin. This is largely because it is a patented isolate and, thus, the research is subsidized by the manufacturers. Over the past two decades there has been an explosion of research regarding this spice and its active ingredients, largely beginning about 2000. Regarding curcumin alone there are some 5500 citations, focusing on its wide-ranging powers as an antioxidant, antitumor, and antiinflammatory agent, with a smaller amount of work being done regarding its antidiabetic, antiaging, and wound healing capacities.

Yet, while less studies have been done on it, there is major proof of medicinal powers of the whole spice form as well. For instance, diets rich in turmeric "stabilize and protect biomolecules in the body at the molecular level..." This is a consequence of its antioxidant and antimutagenic properties. The majority of diseases are induced by a molecular process involving the substance, NF-Kappa Beta. This is a potent protein that promotes within the tissues an abnormal inflammatory response. Excess NF-Kappa Beta can result in arthritis, diabetes, fibromyalgia, heart disease, and cancer. Turmeric and its active ingredients suppress this molecule, preventing it from inducing such diseases.

The absorption issue defined

With the whole food form cooked into food, absorption is not a major issue. There is translocation into the bloodstream, especially when it is cooked in fat. However, the isolated key active ingredients are another issue. These isolates pose a major challenge. This is the issue of impaired absorption, known as poor bioavailability. This is primarily in relation to extracted, single components, like curcumin. Once such a single pigment is removed from the spice, incredibly, the substance becomes more difficult to absorb. What's more, to complicate issues these isolated active principles are rapidly metabolized and eliminated, limiting the therapeutic capacities. This is largely a consequence of their being so isolated, that is they are not held within the natural complex, making them vulnerable to being readily lost. A black pepper extract, piperine, has been evaluated as an adjunct. In one study it increased absorption of curcumin by some 2000%. However, this extract is produced through solvent treatment. As such, it is unnaturally strong and may prove irritating to the digestive tracts of certain people. No one should take such an isolated form of black pepper extract on a regular basis.

There is a safer and, in fact, more effective way of achieving optimal absorption. This is by keeping the curcumin in its own complex, while combining it with all the other major components needed for efficient assimilation. This is why a whole food form of the spice extract is superior to mere isolates alone.

Why is it so difficult to absorb or shall it be said, retain? This is related to the biochemical consequences of turmeric metabolism. Its active ingredients, like curcumin, undergo "rapid metabolism." This leads to the processing of the compounds in the liver by processes known as glucoronidation and sulfation. All this occurs in the liver and results in the rapid dumping of turmeric compounds into the intestines, bound to bile. Once so bound, there is little that can be done to liberate the molecules. So, it is crucial to modulate this to gain the most optimal benefits from this medicine.

Its stubborn degree of absorption explains the use of solvents, since it is insoluble in water, for instance, in digestive juices. Bile, though, does help dissolve it. Obviously, too, it does so readily in petrochemical solvents, like hexane, pentane, acetone, and chloroform. It is also miscible in alcohol, including isopropopanol or rubbing alcohol as well as the edible type, ethyl alcohol or ethanol.

This heavy emphasis on isolating one main ingredient is essentially a disaster. It has been heavily published by a number of investigators that curcumin is surely the active ingredient, despite the fact that there are nearly 100 biologically active substances in this spice. Even so, massive efforts have been made to concentrate and isolate this, essentially to make patented drugs. This proved largely erroneous, as it became clear that through isolation great corruption occurred. The now drug-like curcumin was virtually impossible to absorb in the isolated, standardized form. This is why every effort has been made to attempt to correct this through, as mentioned, the black pepper extract addition and/or adding back the original key compounds, the highly volatile and readily absorbed essential oils. The fact is in nature the essential oils are truly 'essential,' since they render curcumin soluble, largely by dissolving it.

Yet, is natural turmeric really that difficult to utilize? Most of the studies have been done on the isolate. It makes sense that such aberrant chemicals are difficult to both utilize and absorb. Thus, this dilemma has been demonstrated by a number of scientific investigations. In one study after a loading dose of two grams the blood levels of curcumin isolate were virtually undetectable. Yet, when the other previously removed ingredients, such as turmeric essential oil, are added back, absorption was significantly enhanced. The techniques of isolation appear to have more to do with impairing utilization than any other factor.

What is the basis for all this heavy processing? It appears to be largely marketing hype. The entire purpose is to create a drug-like form which can be branded and then sold in a proprietary formula, even if this means the selling of an inferior product. The absorption issue, for instance, was raised by Indian investigators led by A. Vyas. Here, the focus was the creation of patent drugs based on nanotechnology and/or the synthesis of man-made curcumin analogues. In the conclusion of the article the investigators stated that they would invent "new, synthetic analogues" to "overcome the drawbacks of limited bioavailability" and also to deal with "rapid metabolism..." The latter is held as the main factor limiting curcumin's therapeutic powers.

The food form

The food form of turmeric has numerous beneficial powers not found in the heavily processed isolates. This makes sense, since it was the type used in antiquity. This is the kind found in curry powder and turmeric powder. The ideally certified organic raw, whole root or wild roots which are chemical-free is yet another food complex. All these forms of turmeric are medicinal. The ancients used the fresh and powdered root for virtually the exact conditions that the supplement form is prescribed today. There is a good argument for the extensive use of these forms. Regarding the raw root the benefits are obvious being a form of turmeric free of all manipulation and corruption. There isn't even any heat applied to this, unless it is cooked. With raw turmeric, as occurs in CO_2 extracts and the raw root, the molecules are more biologically active than when they are subjected to heat and/or solvents. The powder, too, is minimally processed, only undergoing boiling and heat-based drying.

When buying the dried spice, it is important to search for top-quality sources. These powders must be free of all contaminants and also free of excessive germ levels. Regarding pathogens, this is a major challenge, as, since it is derived from a root, germ levels can be high. Another issue is radiation. This is being used as a medicine, so irradiation is counterproductive, if high-quality, organic, and non-irradiated, all whole food turmeric powders will provide positive results. Yet an additional novel type is the wild turmeric powder, which has a special characteristic versus farm-raised. Whether commercial or organic, wild turmeric has a curcumin content some 25% higher. North American Herb & Spice's TurmaSpice wild turmeric powder and its TurmaMilk triple spice mix, along with Cha's Certified Organic's of Sri Lanka, are examples of such chemical-free, high-potency sources. The TurmaSpice wild turmeric powder has the added benefit of being exceedingly high in turmerones, some 10 times higher than all others. There is another important issue that makes them unique. Both TurmaSpice and TurmaMilk are extensively tested for microbes and have levels well below the requirement. This is because of a special kind of processing unique to these powders, known as dry steam sterilization. To purchase turmeric powder with the highest density of curcumin and turmerones known plus exceptional purity, free of germs, see www.americanwildfoods.com.

Regarding irradiation, this is a real issue. This is because of the commonness of germ-tainting in this spice. So, irradiation of commercial turmeric spice is standard. Yet, there are significant consequences of this. Thermonuclear ions are always residual in irradiated spices and are certainly not conducive to good health. Yet, such residues are only found in low-grade commercial spices, while the privately sourced and packaged type, like TurmaSpice, are free of any such toxins.

The food form offers numerous benefits. It has a pleasant taste and, thus, may be added readily to recipes. It also lends itself to interesting and highly nourishing drinks, using, for instance, raw, whole milk, coconut milk, and/or nut milk as the base, along with other spices and whole food elements. This is known traditionally as Golden Milk or Turmeric Milk, which will be covered later in greater detail.

Raw turmeric root is now commonly available, especially in specialty grocery stores. People should take advantage of it, since it is highly nutritious and health-producing. The whole root contains the following ingredients:

- curcuminoids, about 5%
- essential oils, about 5% to 7%
- fixed oils, like sterols and waxes, about 4%
- resin, about 3%
- protein, about 10%
- fiber, about 5%
- starch, about 50%
- alcohol soluble components, about 14%

Food forms of turmeric have a host of beneficial powers. Extracts of the entire spice have been found in some studies to be more potent as antitumor agents than curcumin alone. In an investigation by A. K. Chakravarty it was found that whole turmeric, extracted with ethanol, was a better antiinflammatory agent than curcumin isolates. It was also found that the whole, complete form was more potent than the isolate at activating lymphocytes for inducing programmed cell death of cancer cell lines. This led the investigators to say the incredible, which was to "recommend it (that is the whole food form) over curcumin whenever possible."

It was researchers publishing in the *Journal of Food and Nutrition Research* who made similar findings, discovering that the antioxidant capacities of turmeric were greater than for curcumin alone. In the ability to inhibit oxidative damage, once again, whole food turmeric extract was the winner, being some 15 times greater than curcumin alone, a significant, in fact, monumental difference. This proves that man-made forms of turmeric are invariably feeble compared to the complete, unprocessed, whole food types.

Antioxidant powers

This is often a neglected element of turmeric's medicinal powers, as the emphasis has been on its antiinflammatory capacities. The blocking of oxidative damage is essential for the achievement of optimal health and for the prevention of disease. It is one of the keys for reversing and curing disease processes. No doubt, turmeric spice is a potent antioxidant, although its most powerful component in this regard is curcumin. Turmeric antioxidants scavenge free radicals, molecules in the body that cause cell damage, while accelerating the aging process. Unchecked, free radicals readily damage cell membranes and even more direly, the DNA itself, the latter being devastating.

It makes sense. Pigment-rich, turmeric is like a coating; for example, it stains not only, for instance, clothing or the skin but also the cells and organs within the body. In particular, this pigment stains the fatty tissues, to which it readily adheres, imparting its antioxidant capacity directly.

The stained tissue now is more stable to oxidation. Moreover, it is capable of permeating all tissue, especially those made up largely of fat. This is why it is so invaluable as a treatment for disorders related to cognitive decline such as dementia and Alzheimer's disease. It also explains its capacity to halt inflammation, that is by, essentially, soaking up the free radicals as they attempt to attack the cell membranes.

The antioxidant powers of all spices are significant, with turmeric being one of the top of these. Other exceedingly powerful ones include cloves, wild oregano, wild rosemary, and cumin as well as cinnamon. A most therapeutic approach is to combine such antioxidant-rich spices, which creates a synergistic capacity that is immense.

The ORAC of turmeric can be confusing. This is because there is one level for supplements and yet another for the raw spice and/or dried, ground spice. For antioxidant measurements the ground spice has been the most well researched. According to USDA documents it has a total ORAC of approximately 1300 per gram. There are two ORAC levels, the water-phase one and the lipid soluble element. Turmeric scores highest on the lipid-phase antioxidant at some 830 per gram, while the water-phase component is 450 per gram. Compare this to wild oregano, which scores exceedingly high in the water phase at 1650, while lower in the fat phase at 225. That's why the two together in supplement form or in spice mixes is ideal.

Even so, turmeric itself is exceedingly potent, the spice powder having an ORAC level of nearly 128,000 per 100 grams. Oregano is even higher at 175,000 per 100 grams, while the ORAC of sumac outer bran is 312,000 and dried rosemary, up to 170,000 per 100 grams. Cinnamon powder comes in slightly higher than turmeric at 131,000 per 100 grams, therefore the logic combining these, as in TurmaMilk spice mix. Sumac bran, as found in OregaMax capsules, and ground cloves are the most powerful high-ORAC foods known. Curiously, traditionally, two of the most aggressive antioxidant foods, wild oregano and wild *Rhus coriaria,* that is sumac, have been combined for centuries in Mediterranean village formulas. The logic of the highly regarded whole food supplement containing these components, raw OregaMax capsules, is now confirmed.

Even so, the antioxidant powers of turmeric and its extracts largely account for its therapeutic powers. Free radicals are aggressive and readily damage the cell membranes as well as its nucleus. Turmeric blocks this, with the turmerones and curcumin taking the lead as active, antioxidant components. After turmeric or its key components are administered, there is a noticeable reduction in free radical generation, including a drop in nitric oxide production. The fact is all great inflammatory reactions are mediated by toxic, destructive free radicals. Turmeric mops these up, which explains its efficacy in the treatment and reversal of arthritis, hardening of the arteries, cancer, diabetes, respiratory diseases, liver disorders, stomach diseases, neurodegenerative conditions, and pancreatic ailments. In a review of all the available scientific literature a conclusion can be made. Turmeric, an entirely GRAS substance, an actual food additive, is highly effective against inflammatory and degenerative diseases, largely because of its antioxidant powers.

Chapter Three

Whole Food Turmeric Therapy

The use of the whole turmeric spice is a reliable means to gain the immense benefits of this invaluable natural medicine. Whole food forms include the complete, natural root, the whole, minimally processed turmeric powder, and certain high quality dietary supplements.

Does this mean that adding turmeric and/or curry powder to the food is a cure? To a degree this is the case. It surely is exceedingly health-giving to consume the unprocessed whole. In one study it was found that people who do so in even modest amounts, for instance, once or twice per month have less dementia and Alzheimer's disease than those who don't. In larger quantities, though, in many ways it truly is a cure. Perhaps people love curries for reasons much more than mere taste. They unwittingly realize that curried food digests well and, in fact, stimulates overall digestion. They may also experience mood elevation, although rarely realizing the source. People crave curried or turmeric-spiced food, and the reason for this is becoming increasingly clear. Furthermore, food, herbs, and spices are truly God's natural means of healing and curing humanity of the most common and severe ailments.

An effort should be made to use this spice in the traditional fashion. Thus, meat dishes should be ideally spiced with turmeric and/or curry powder, as this will dramatically aid in all aspects of the digestive process. The same is true, if possible, of vegetable dishes, including those which are baked and or skillet-cooked but, particularly, those in which there are considerable amounts of fat such as the fat of meat, poultry, and coconut. If at all possible, as do many Indo-Pakistanis, add curry or turmeric powder to all egg dishes, including omelets and quiche recipes.

Golden Milk: drink of the heavens?

A true, ancient Ayurvedic tradition, Golden Milk has been used for centuries as a rejuvenating beverage. The word "Golden" obviously derives from the turmeric coloration. For purposes of this book it will be mainly known as turmeric milk. In particular, it has been consumed for joint pain and stiffness. It has also been relied upon to improve overall flexibility as well as vitality. Regular consumers experience an increased ability to move about more fluidly, which is known in Indian lore as "lubrication." There is more bounce in the step and a greater degree of overall vigor. Once again, in Indian culture to achieve these benefits the drug form was never used and, rather, this was strictly a result of the intake of the whole food form, though through a special means of administration.

Instinctively, it would seem, the local people knew the issue, which is that the turmeric active components are poorly absorbed. Thus, they emulsified them in a milk base through heating and through the addition of absorption aids, like ginger, cinnamon, and black pepper as well as various fats.

The ultimate turmeric milk is that made by cooking it into the milk substance. The milk emulsifies the turmeric. In other words, it renders it soluble, so it can be more readily absorbed into the bloodstream. The addition of extra fat, such as ghee, unrefined sesame oil, organic butter, and/or coconut fat, further increases its assimilation. In the home kitchen for making a heavily emulsified milk the ultimate source is raw, whole milk or organic milk, although nut milks also work well. Nut milk options include almond, cashew, hemp, macadamia nut, and filbert. The fat base will create the necessary mycellization to force the issue of absorption. Freshly ground black pepper can be added as this, too, stimulates a higher level of absorption. So does fresh ginger juice or ginger powder, which is equally as effective as black pepper. For purging pain and inflammation such a milk may prove just as effective as isolate-based supplements, in fact, in some cases more so.

Turmeric milk can be made with the whole spice powder and/or the freshly juiced root substance. Here is a simplistic recipe for its production:

Standard turmeric milk recipe

one cup nut or whole, organic milk
1 or 1½ tsp. whole food organic or wild turmeric powder
dash or two black pepper
dash or two ground cardamom (optional)
raw, unprocessed honey or yacon syrup to taste, add after taking off heat
½ tsp. sesame oil or ghee (or a tsp. of organic butter), added after removing from heat
water, as needed

Simmer turmeric and black pepper in water until it forms a nice paste, about eight minutes, adding more water, if necessary. Meanwhile, heat the milk. Before it boils, remove from heat. Combine the two mixtures using a blender if desired. Add raw honey or organic, raw yacon syrup to taste. The cardamom may be cooked with the turmeric for added flavor.

An optional recipe is to use the fresh juice of turmeric root. The root juices well, and the liquor is highly flavorful. There is less residue in the pan with the fresh root compared to the typical powder; use two teaspoonsful or more of the juice as a replacement.

Yet another excellent recipe involves the addition of ginger, once again, either as an organic, non-irradiated powder or the fresh juice. Per cup, add a quarter teaspoon of the powder or a teaspoon of the fresh root juice.

Let us review other ways to make this golden treat using a few additional delicious additives without making the pre-paste additive:

Doctor's Own Homemade, Extra-Rich Turmeric Milk

This formula is far more potent than the standard type and is actually a natural drug-like golden/turmeric milk. For this always use organic nut, coconut, or cow's milk. Regardless of the milk base that is used it is delicious and heart-, as well as joint,-warming:

1½ cups unsweetened almond milk
½ cup unsweetened macadamia nut milk (or other unsweetened nut milk or even organic whole cow's milk)
2 or 3 tsp. organic and/or wild turmeric powder
½ tsp. organic ginger powder
1 tsp. organic cinnamon powder from the original Ceylon type (if not available, use regular cinnamon, ½ tsp.)

Note: instead of these three spices, individually, you can use 3 tsp. TurmaMilk triple spice mix

tsp. freshly expressed juice of organic turmeric root
tsp. freshly expressed juice of organic ginger root
a few seeds from cardamom pods (an optional but taste-tantalizing addition)
raw, unprocessed honey or organic yacon syrup to taste after taking off
   of heat
2 tsp. ghee or cold-pressed sesame oil, for instance, Sesam-E, to stir in
   after heating

Note: if you wish to make this less potent, add an additional cup of nut milk or even thin with filtered water

Warm over low heat, stirring to mix thoroughly. The purpose of this extra strong type is to increase the powers of the milk as an antiinflammatory drink. The macadamia nut milk is a delicious addition and helps emulsify turmeric's active ingredients even further, as does the richer addition of ghee or sesame oil.

An optional method is to blend the milk in the blender after heating to meld flavors. Sometimes, this is necessary, since there is a tendency for a sediment to form and for ideal benefits this should be emulsified into the milk.

No doubt, regardless of how it is made, that is with the milk from nuts, coconut, or organic cow's/goat's milk, this is both nutritious and delicious, while also being highly medicinal. The addition of coconut milk and/or oil offers further therapeutic powers as well as a luscious taste. The coconut fat helps drive turmeric's active ingredients right into the lymph and bloodstream.

Coconut milk/fat is itself a natural medicine. Some 50% of the fat in the oil is lauric acid, one of the most digestible fats known. The body thrives on this fatty acid, readily absorbing it. Upon digestion, it is converted to monolaurin, an antiseptic-like fatty acid. This fatty acid has the capacity to dissolve the outer coating of certain viruses, destroying them. It also has actions against certain bacteria as well as parasites.

Lauric acid and monolaurin are known as medium-chain triglycerides. They are virtually immediately digested, rapidly crossing into the bloodstream and lymph. They are also readily utilized as energy by the internal organs, notably the liver, heart, and kidneys. Medium chain fatty acids suppress excessive appetite and contribute to weight loss. Yet, they act in the opposite fashion as well, facilitating weight gain in the debilitated and weak. Coconut milk also contains these fatty acids, while being a good source of vitamin E, B vitamins, phosphorus, iron, and magnesium.

Golden Coconut Spice Milk

2 cups organic coconut milk
1 tsp. coconut fat (optional)
1½ tsp. organic and/or wild turmeric powder or 2 tsp. fresh expressed juice—or, two tsp. TurmaMilk spice mix
½ tsp. true cinnamon powder
¼ tsp. nutmeg (optional)
one-inch piece raw, organic ginger, peeled and grated
raw, unprocessed honey or raw yacon syrup to taste, if desired

In a saucepan heat all ingredients, except honey or yacon and whisk. Convert to medium heat until it just bubbles. Turn down heat to very low, and simmer for five minutes or so until the flavors meld; strain out any ginger or other particles (or leave in, if desired).

For numerous other turmeric milk recipe ideas see the recipe section of this book. In this regard the use of TurmaMilk pre-mix makes this easier. Made with a combination of high-turmerone wild turmeric plus organic, true cinnamon and organic ginger. It is in the ideal ratio to make a delicious, medicinal drink. To order see www.americanwildfoods.com or check high-quality health food stores.

Benefits of drinking turmeric milk

The benefits of drinking this milk are truly immense. The active ingredients in fully emulsified turmeric drink aid the function of all cells of the body, especially immune, endocrine, liver, digestive, and renal cells. This is through the action of the turmeric active ingredients on a wide range of systems, including liver detoxification, kidney purification, and gene expression. Moreover, turmeric offers that novel cleansing power of promoting healthy cell function while also destroying cancer cells. It also has the property of anti-angiogenesis, meaning it helps block the development of the additional blood supply necessary for cancer cell growth as well as the growth of the skin lesions of psoriasis and eczema.

It would appear that turmeric, especially in an emulsified form, is a broad-spectrum anti-cancer agent. In other words, it helps the body purge itself of virtually any kind of cancerous growth and/or tumor, although its effectiveness is enhanced by other spice-based complexes, like wild oregano, rosemary, and sage. Furthermore, turmeric is aided in this power through simultaneous consumption of ginger and/or its extracts.

According to the available clinical studies the regular intake of absorbable turmeric and, in particular, well-absorbed curcumin leads to the following beneficial actions:

- healthier cholesterol levels
- prevention of the oxidation of LDL cholesterol
- maintenance of healthy HDL cholesterol levels
- prevention of sudden onset myocardial infarction
- prevention of excessive stickiness of platelets
- suppression of the development of pre-diabetic metabolic syndrome
- easing arthritic symptoms, including stiffness
- suppression of stress-induced tumor formation
- blockade of viral replication in chronic viral syndromes
- protection against toxin-induced liver or kidney damage
- increased secretion of bile
- protection against lung damage from exposure to toxins
- protection against skin aging and rejuvenation of the skin
- prevention of the degeneration of the brain and nerves

These are many of the expected benefits of the regular consumption of turmeric milk. Therefore, clearly, this drink is full-body protection against the major degenerative diseases. Even so, there are many other unanticipated ones such as an improvement in overall digestion. Inflammation within the stomach and, particularly, colon is eased. There is often an easing, even reversal, of hemorrhoids. The skin and eyes become more vital. Moreover, now, it is possible to make it even more potent with the addition of wild turmeric powder, which is both potent in active ingredients and delicious in taste. Through turmeric therapy the world does become a finer, better place. There is in addition to the disease-related benefits an improvement in the senses: in sight, taste, hearing, and smell. These are the 'side effects' from regular consumption of turmeric milk and/or whole food turmeric powder.

Whole food hemp: a turmeric synergist?

In the history of India two plants stand out as universal medicines, which are utilitarian for a wide range of diseases. These are turmeric and cannabis. Today, cannabis is available from not only marijuana but also industrial hemp, the latter being a 'legal' source of the cannabis active ingredients. Whole food hemp stalk extract, as it is known, a rich source of substances known as phytocannabinoids, as well as biologically active terpenes, can play a major role as an antiinflammatory agent. Thus, it would work in concert with the turmeric whole food components. Hemp stalk extract is rich in two key groups of compounds which compliment the turmeric, notably the cannabinoids and terpenes.

Regarding cannabinoids, hemp, or cannabis, is the richest source. These substances, which include cannabidiol—also known as CBD—among 80 other substances, feed the body's endocannabinoid system, which is necessary for modulating pain and inflammation. It is like the opiate system, that is it exists to specifically interact with powerful, naturally occurring chemicals. Hemp or cannabis stalk is also a dense source of a key group of novel antiinflammatory compounds, known as terpenes, particularly that invaluable, highly potent one, Beta-caryophyllene. It is this compound which acts as a vigorous dietary cannabinoid for fighting inflammation and pain. As well, the cannabinoids aid in mood elevation, while also acting as powerful anti-seizure and anti-spasmodic agents. The combination of turmeric and hemp known as Canacurmin is recommended for a variety of conditions. The name stands for a fact that this is a complex of turmeric active ingredients and whole food components, along with the full complex of whole food hemp stalk biological substances. It is for the first time in history a supplemental complex combining two of the most powerful anti-pain and anti-inflammation natural medicines known. Canacurmin has all of the active ingredients found in Turmeric-PLUS combined with organic, supercritically extracted hemp stalk extract and is available as 500 mg gelcaps or as sublingual drops. The fact is the combination of this is double action, where the curcuminoids, turmerones, and cannabinoids plus hemp terpenes greatly support a healthy response to inflammation, while also fighting injury-related pain. It also has a power, this joint complex, to combat neurological disorders while stalling the aging process.

Chapter Four

Isolates, Concentrates, and More

On the market today there are countless brands of turmeric supplements. How, then, is the individual to determine which of these brands is most powerful and effective as well as the safest for long-term use? What is little known is that the majority of these supplements are extensively altered. The issue of molecular manipulation should not be taken lightly. In their short-sightedness scientists believe that they can dramatically improve upon nature by grossly altering the natural balance. Yet, the ultimate goal is not merely to create a purportedly more potent version but, in fact, to produce a patentable product which can be marketed as an exclusive.

In the world of turmeric supplements most of them are highly similar. There is a global effort in the pharmaceutical circles to make super-concentrates, mainly in the form of isolated curcumin. So, what is commonly done? The curcumin pigment is aggressively extracted from turmeric raw material. Then, it is processed further to make a concentrate. In order to isolate/concentrate it emulsifiers are added or used, including rather noxious ones, many of which are GMO-tainted. The list of emulsifying agents added to curcumin supplements is as follows:

- propylethylene glycol
- biopolymers
- cellulose
- corn oil
- hydrogel complexes
- liposome complexes
- nanoparticles
- soy lecithin and its derivatives

Do people really want to consume such substances or chemical compounds with their medicinal turmeric extracts? There are also a number of so-called super-molecular complexes being used, including "supermolecular assemblies of curcumin with cyclodextrins and curcubyturyl..." Of note, the dextrins are derivatives of GMO-tainted corn. Through these agents the objective is to enhance the notoriously poor absorption of curcumin through, notes K. I. Priyadarsini in "The Chemistry of Curcumin from Extraction to Therapeutic Agent," rendering it soluble and then entrapping it "in hydrophobic pockets..."

The highly experimental nano-compounds are also used to alter absorption. These are known as "mesoporous silica nanoparticles." Such particles are wholly synthetic and are, thus, entirely unknown in nature. Even gold particle-based nanoparticles are used in curcumin formulations. The gold particles are aberrant, being altered from non-toxic, naturally occurring gold to nano-molecules. The gold particles then purportedly bind to curcumin molecules, altering their structure. Clearly, then, through the use of such emulsifiers the turmeric extract becomes nothing other than a pharmaceutical drug, a potentially dangerous one at that.

This is all done to rectify what is nothing other than an industrial disaster. The investigators discovered, unexpectedly, that their patent curcumin isolates are notoriously difficult to absorb. As demonstrated by scientific studies it takes great doses, often repeated throughout the day, to achieve even minor blood levels. There was no intention by the makers, originally, to manipulate absorption. That's because they presumed the isolate would be superior to the whole food form. The forced attempts are a consequence of the failed bioavailability. Yet, an initial blunder cannot be corrected by another artificial, desperate intervention. The fact is as a result of all such manipulations the majority of turmeric's medicinal properties are lost.

There may be a degree of antiinflammatory powers, which remain. People suffer desperately, so any positive action will be noticed. Yet, what is lost is the spice's wholesomeness, its varied and diverse features: the ones responsible for the simultaneous prevention and reversal of numerous diseases, which is what makes turmeric so unique.

Manipulating the science

Today, turmeric-based supplements are big-money. It seems that every innovative scientist is attempting to create or patent a new version, all through making highly altered extracts. Greed enters the equation and, thus, data is manipulated for financial gain. Studies don't seem to address the primary issue, which is just how much more effective are the patented extracts or concentrates versus whole or minimally processed forms.

Because of the desire to be the 'lead' or "number-one" product there is temptation for corruption. This includes the gross manipulation of scientific studies. No doubt, virtually any turmeric-based supplement will have a degree of efficacy. Yet, how truly effective are they? How well are these products really absorbed? Moreover, how much of it is placebo effect versus reality?

Thus, many such supplements will be analyzed, especially those making extensive claims. Are such claims real, or is it just marketing hype? This is not always easy to determine. The majority of the marketing claims are based on absorption, not so much clinical efficacy. Let us, then, see how many of these claims are truly justified and/or substantiated.

Meriva

A patented formulation of curcumin this is a typical example of a turmeric isolate. Here, the final product is made using GMOs, in this case, soy lecithin. In fact, such large amounts of lecithin are used that it is two parts of this GMO to one part curcumin. This is purportedly to emulsify it and render the molecule more absorbable. This is why Meriva is called "a patented delivery form of curcumin." Yet, there are such a wide array of additives and excipients in the supplemental ingredients that the final content of curcumin is only "around 20%." Other published ingredients include phosphatidylcholine complex, as already indicated, that is a specific form of lecithin, the amino acid leucine, and calcium citrate. Clearly, then, the raw material contains a massive amount of GMOs. Furthermore, despite the attempts to modify absorption through GM emulsifiers the Meriva complex is one of the most poorly absorbed of all, proving the futility of synthetically-based, forced absorption. It also proves the corruption of using genetically engineered ingredients in an attempt to manipulate nature.

BCM-95

Made by an Indian biotech company, DolCas Biotech, BCM-95 is a patented formula of turmeric active ingredients touted as a combination of curcuminoids and essential oils. The formula is based on the premise that the levels of these chemicals in the root are "naturally very low" and so, when concentrated, this makes a more clinically effective formula. This is a "standardized" supplement, meaning the exceedingly high levels of curcuminoids and essential oils are artificial. It also contains phospholipids. The claim is, though, that it is made of 100% turmeric extract components. It is 86% curcuminoids plus 7% to 9% essential oils. Yet another standardized formula available from this firm is Turmeric-95, which is standardized to "95% curcuminoids" but does not contain the essential oils.

Even so, what is BCM-95, that is what does it mean? Does it mean that each capsule or tablet is 95% curcumin, or does it mean 95% curcuminoids? Or, does it imply that the finished powder patented by the company is of this concentration? Then, what does the other 5% consist of?

One supplement that is based on this patented complex is Curamin. The product combines BCM-95 with a host of other extracts, including those from boswellia, a type of frankincense, and the enzyme nattokinase. For the purist this poses an issue, since this enzyme is derived from genetically engineered soy. The amino acid DLPA or DL-phenylalanine is also added, which is an entirely synthetic substance. It is currently produced through bacterial synthesis using genetically altered E. coli.

The frankincense extract is trade named BosPure, which is an ethyl acetate extract. The chemical used for extraction is synthetic; in other words, it is not organic and is the same one largely used to extract BCM-95 curcuminoids. Regarding the boswellia or frankincense component according to the label claim it is made by standardization through "reducing beta-boswellic acid" and then manipulating the active ingredients, providing "higher levels of AKBA," a different form of the compound."

BCM-95 has the disadvantages of relatively poor absorption, along with GMO infestation. Moreover, there is the significant issue of the lack of using organic ingredients as well as the addition of a synthetic amino acid made through bioengineering. Even the label admits the presence of GMOs in the form of "soy particles." This is essentially a disclaimer for those who have known soy allergies. Furthermore, the potency of the BCM-95 curcumin is difficult to assess, because of the presence in the formula of other antiinflammatory agents, notably soy-derived nattokinase and standardized frankincense.

According to the company Website the solvents used in its production are "only ethanol or ethyl acetate." Regarding the latter it is a hazardous material used in paint, laquer, and fingernail polish manufacture and must be handled carefully. Excessive exposure via ingestion, inhalation, and/or skin exposure can prove poisonous. If only ethanol is used, ideally organic in source, this would be the least noxious of all solvents.

There are many people who report beneficial effects of the BCM-95 preparation. Yet, the presence of GMOs in this formulation poses significant concerns of the potential for long-term toxicity. Moreover, there can be no ultimate benefit from the intake of hard, pressed pills. The absorption of curcumin from such pressed pills is exceedingly poor. This will compromise overall results in disease reversal.

Ideally, the makers of BCM-95 should make some adaptations. At a minimum they must purge this highly popular supplement of GMOs. The fact is tens of thousands of people take this supplement. Do they realize that with every dose they are ingesting components of GM soy?

Super BioCurcumin

Made by Life Extension this is yet another brand based on the patented BCM-95 isolate. The ingredient list of the formulation is as follows: BCM-95 Bio-Curcumin turmeric 25 to one extract, standardized to 95% curcuminoids complexed with essential oils. Other ingredients include vegetable cellulose, along with stearic acid and silica. Vegetable cellulose may be a way to hide the source, which is often genetically modified corn.

A caution is listed on the label, as follows:

Do not take if you have gallbladder problems or gallstones.

Like Curamin, this is a pharmaceutical-style dietary supplement, its absorption and potency being heavily compromised by extensive processing. Perhaps this is why the gallbladder warning is found on the label, since whole food turmeric is a powerful gallbladder supporting agent and does not cause any untoward reactions.

Theracurmin

Claiming to be yet another example of a scientific breakthrough in curcumin technology, Theracurmin is yet another highly processed dietary supplement. The solvent-extracted curcumin is solubilized within vegetable gum, known as gum ghatti. Next, this complex is ground to produce "microscopic particles" that are purportedly "100 times smaller than regular curcumin powder." For the size of the capsule the amount of curcumin is relatively low, only 30 mg. This means the remainder is mere agents from components other than turmeric. This is essentially an attempt to create, once again, 'forced absorption of a compound that, on its own, is virtually impossible to be utilized.

Produced by Theravalues Corp. like the others, Theracumin is a patented raw material. This is, then, purchased by supplement companies, which market it under their own trade names. The major seller of this, Natural Factors, with its product CurcuminRich, per its label claim holds it as a "natural preparation that utilizes advanced techniques to reduce the particle size of curcumin...to dramatically increase its solubility and bioavailability." According to the label "Theracurmin is the best-absorbed form of curcumin on the market." This is said despite the fact that the company has not tested all the supplements available. Other ingredients include magnesium stearate, silica, and croscarmellose sodium. Like BCM-95, none of the sources for raw materials are organic. Nor, in particular, is the raw material certified to be grown free of pesticides and herbicides.

What isn't mentioned on the label is the various excipients used in manufacture, which are in the end product. As described by A. Imaizumi in PharmaNutrition these components include a variety of GMO-tainted substances, including corn starch, dextrin, citric acid, and maltose, all of which are largely from GM corn.

C3 Curcumin Complex

Yet another patented product, in this case made by Sabinsa, Curcumin C3 is, essentially, isolated, purified curcumin. The final material is a combination of the extracted curcumin plus a patented component of black pepper, known as BioPerine. The subject of a number of clinical trials it has been tested against colorectal cancer, lichen planus, precancerous skin lesions, and in the prevention, as well as treatment, of Alzheimer's disease. It's made by a rather extensive chemical process, which includes the following procedures:

- solvent extraction
- concentration
- freezing the concentrate to create crystals
- repeating these processes until gaining the desired purity and potency

The solvents used in its production per its patent filing include acetone and ethyl acetate, with residual levels as high as 1000 or more ppm. According to the filing the turmeric is washed 'repeatedly in either acetone or ethyl acetate' until the curcuminoids are extracted. Brands using this include Jarrow, with its Curcumin 95, Doctor's Best, and VitaCost. Once again, it must be kept in mind that the curcuminoids are merely one of many elements, no more than 5%, of the entire turmeric complex. The isolation of this alone restricts the wide-ranging benefits available from the whole food complex. The C3 Complex consists of only three of the countless dozens of turmeric components and is particularly devoid of the naturally occurring essential oil complex, the turmerone group, so necessary for optimal utilization. Regardless, ethyl acetate and/or acetone extracts, with residual chemical levels, are less than ideal as turmeric supplements. Moreover, they should, in particular, not be used as the preferred types for cancer victims, who are ultrasensitive to chemical solvents. The fact is such solvent residues may activate cancerous tissue by damaging protective cell membranes.

Turmeric-Curcumin

A number of supplements have such a listing on the label. No one seems to know what this means. Upon careful inspection of the label, often, it is found that this represents a combination of turmeric powder with isolated curcumin. Many of these supplements labeled with this brand contain solvent-extracted black pepper as an adjuvant. Allergic intolerance to this spice is common, and, thus, it is a less than ideal routine additive to turmeric supplements. For those who are ultra-sensative to black pepper, in fact, ginger is equally effective as an adjuvant to stimulate improved absorption.

CurcuWin

Made by OmniActive Health Technologies CurcuWin is a highly purified curcumin extract that is blended with antioxidants, in this case, commercial vitamin E and/or vitamin C. This is then bound to a starch-based carrier. The starchy carrier described is maltodextrin. After this, it is blended with fatty acids.

The technology used is its own patented UltraSOL Nutrient Technology. This is acclaimed as a "molecular dispersion process that enhances the solubility and bioavailability" of the fat soluble elements of the drug. It is also said that the encapsulated powder is 20% turmeric-based matter, notably the curcuminoids, the rest of which is additives. Obviously, then, numerous non-turmeric elements are found in the final product, which is surely less than desirable. In fact, some 80% of the mass is carrier molecules.

The patented system is listed as "beadlet technology," where the beadlets act as a "coating system." It is patented as "OmniBead." Who in the world would consume such a highly altered, primarily synthetic supplement? There is no way to achieve the ultimate, widespread benefits of turmeric by doing so.

Biomor Curcumin

Biomor Curcumin purports to be an improvement over the standard isolate-based supplements on the basis that it is free of toxic solvents. In particular, the emphasis in promotional literature is that it is free of a highly poisonous chlorinated hydrocarbon, ethylene dichloride or EDC. Like numerous others, the purveyors claim to use standardized material as the active principle, so-called 95% curcumin or curcuminoids. Company literature also states that this formula is, again, patented and that it is "a new, patented manufacturing process that dramatically increases blood plasma curcumin levels" beyond any other.

It is, though, an extensively manipulated supplement, where orchestrated levels of curcumin and essential oils are created. Furthermore, it is stated in the info sheet that this is 95% "purified" curcumin and that, somehow, it beats all others, since it is absorbed twice as well as competitors. In fact, the claim is that the absorption is 8-fold greater than other products claiming to be 95% curcumin. However, it is not stated precisely how this 8-fold greater absorption has been determined.

MetaCurcumin

Produced by RevGenetics, MetaCurcumin is touted as a significantly more well absorbed curcumin than all others. This is a nanotechnology form of turmeric, which is heavily processed. Each serving, it is claimed, provides up to 23 grams of standardized curcumin. Despite the claims of enhanced absorption the real issue is the gross manipulation of the end product. Clearly, in this case the supplement is tainted extensively with nanoparticles, likely made from gold molecules. Such nanoparticles are associated with an increased risk for a variety of health disorders. The particles are particularly toxic to the lungs, increasing the risks for asthma, bronchitis, emphysema, and lung cancer. Of note, there is also nano-silver, which has been directly associated with cellular toxicity.

Consider the work of investigators at the University of Southern Denmark. First to bring the dangers of nano-silver to light, they discovered that such particles, as found in cosmetics and dietary supplements, as well as in some food packaging, aggressively penetrate the cells, where they wreak havoc. Silver itself, they note, is not exceedingly toxic by itself. However, when it is broken down into nano-particles, it becomes aggressive, entering human cells, where it causes alterations. The investigators examined human intestinal cells exposed to nano-particles, and their findings were telling. "Nano-silver," they said, "leads to the formation of harmful...free radicals in cells." There are also, they determined, derogatory "changes in the form and amounts of proteins," a cause for significant "worry." Therefore, by no means can nanoparticle-based nutritional supplements be deemed safe for human consumption. Moreover, they have never been tested to prove safety. No one should consume such supplements. There is no need to do so. Whole food turmeric extracts are superior in efficacy, plus they are free of all nano-particles.

Curcupure

Curcupure appears to offer a benefit over other isolated supplements, since the raw material utilized is certified organic. Even so, it is still a heavily processed isolate, based upon the 95% curcuminoid technology. The claim is that it is based on a process deemed "microencapsulation." Yet, there is little to no information on just how this microencapsulation is achieved. Surely, it involves the addition of substances foreign to the turmeric complex. No patent is available for Curcupure, so it is virtually impossible to determine how it is made. Even so, it has the same dilemma associated with other purified curcumin supplements of difficult absorption. This is a consequence of the use of solvents plus GMO-tainted emulsifiers, which alter, destructively, the nature of the turmeric complex.

Longview Optimized Curcumin

This formula is advertised as containing curcumin that is "optimized for maximum targeting...into the blood and tissues." The Website claims it was developed by "an elite group of university neuroscientists" from UCLA. The claim is that it is some 65% more bioavailable than "unformulated curcumin," their basing this on contrary testing with other brands. To make this raw material purified curcumin particles are mixed with emulsifiers, known medically as lipophilic compounds. The curcumin is surrounded by these emulsifiers, purportedly for the purpose of making it more readily absorbed into the bloodstream.

Images of the final material demonstrate that it is highly refined and altered, bearing little to no resemblance of natural, whole food turmeric powder.

Turmeric-PLUS (formerly Turmerol)

Turmeric-PLUS is unique compared to all other supplements. It is a complete turmeric complex, which is entirely different from the typical high-powered isolates. In addition, it is completely novel in regard to its source. This supplement is made exclusively from certified organic wild turmeric, which grows in refuge areas near national parks and other forested areas. In contrast to other turmeric sources pesticides and herbicides are never used on these plants. As a natural medicine wild-growing plants are much more potent than their farm-raised cousins. When collected, wild turmeric has a larger, more dense, and more colorful, primary root than the farm-raised types. Regarding curcumin content it has been determined that wild turmeric is up to 3% higher than other varieties, having up to 6% curcumin by weight, which is unheard of in all managed varieties, even organic.

For this potent product two different extraction methods are utilized. Supercritical extraction is used to pull out the essential oils as well as the terpenes and waxes. To extract the curcuminoids an organic ethanol-based method is applied. The final complex is known as the oleoresin fraction. What is unique about this supplement is that only certified organic alcohol is used to make this complex, which puts Turmeric-PLUS in a league by itself. No other chemicals of any kind are used, including isopropyl alcohol, hexane, ethylene dichloride, or acetone. Thus, in the case of Turmeric-PLUS there is full transparency,

The other unique aspect relates to its rawness. Turmeric-PLUS contains raw forms of the spice's elements. This is because its major fraction, the essential oils and fixed fats, is CO_2-extracted. Delicate molecules, these essential oil components, the turmerones, are most potent in the raw state. The other component, the turmeric oleoresin, the one rich in curcuminoids, is not raw, because heat must be applied to drive off the alcohol medium. Yet, the curcuminoids are not as sensitive to heat as are the turmerones and, thus, remain highly biologically active.

Yet another novelty is the freeness of this supplement of all synthetics. In contrast to the various isolates no GMOs of any kind are used. Nor are there any added nanoparticles and/or emulsifiers. Moreover, Turmeric-PLUS undergoes no purification processes of any kind. Nor are any of its biological ingredients isolated. It is a true, whole food form of turmeric extract with the full variety of active ingredients, all in a balance the same as that found in nature. Because it has the full complex of turmeric substances it is readily absorbed into the bloodstream.

There is another issue regarding this that sets it apart from all others. This relates to the environment. This is an eco-friendly supplement. It is also rather than pharmaceutically produced or mass synthesized a family-style production. Rather than produced in a corporate environment it is all under the control of a biodynamic farmer, who organizes the picking and extracting. Local villagers are hired to pick the turmeric from the wild, which is, then, carefully processed in a cooperative facility. As well in the final supplements there is an effort at conservation. Unlike virtually all other tumeric supplements no box is used in the packaging, which saves, environmentally, on tree harvesting.

The independent reviews of this supplement are exceedingly impressive. Typically, evaluators have stated it is the most potent turmeric extract available and that, essentially, no other turmeric or curcumin supplement can remotely compare to its medicinal powers. Some of these case histories, based upon written testimonials from people suffering from pain syndromes or disease process, are as follows:

- immediate relief for a chronic pain syndrome that makes it difficult for chiropractic adjustments; now, the adjustments can be made more effectively
- the elimination of the use of the arthritis medication Celebrex through the intake of just 500 mg daily; the same patient also halted all use of Tylenol and Advil
- reversal of a horrific case of chronic sciatic in one month through using wild, raw turmeric sublingual drops
- the purging of a number of the inflammatory symptoms of late stage Lyme using the liquid form as sublingual drops
- the elimination of generalized joint and muscular pain in late-stage Lyme disease

One patient reported that it aided greatly in reversing intestinal issues, "dramatically decreasing the inflammation" that existed within the gut, while the standard types of curcumin supplements could not achieve this. Still another reported the following: "Through taking the Turmeric-PLUS I gained a considerable amount of flexibility in my joints through reduction of inflammation."

Available as BSE-free gelatin capsules Turmeric-PLUS is the only guaranteed whole food plus high potency

Curcuma longa supplement available. It is also guaranteed not to be manipulated, chemically, for enhanced absorption. Additionally, it is in a league by itself, since it is 100% wild, as well as certified organic, while also containing dozens of components in a non-heated, that is raw, state. This is the least processed and altered of all turmeric supplements. It also contains a wider range of the spice's active ingredients than any other. Finally, there is a turmeric supplement that is free of all corruptions and can, thus, be taken with impunity. None of the typical petrochemical solvents are used, whether acetone, methane, and/or dichloroethane, the latter two being chlorinated hydrocarbons.

Canacurmin: synergy-plus

There is another environmentally friendly, non-toxic form of turmeric supplement available. Known as Canacurmin it is a complex of raw and traditionally extracted wild turmeric plus raw, supercritical cannabis stalk extract. The cannabis extract formula also varies in containing sesame oil, which is a traditional Ayurvedic base oil. The turmeric in Canacurmin is in the same dosage and type as found in Turmeric-PLUS.

It has already been described how the turmeric found in Turmeric-PLUS is made. Yet, what process is used for the hemp/cannabis stalk extract? How is it environmentally healthy? In fact, the hemp stalks used are from plants grown organically in northern Europe. The top of the plant is used for fiber, while the remainder is harvested and then processed. This is through supercritical extraction. Thus, no chemicals of any kind are used. Nor is heat applied. This means that the full compliment of cannabis active ingredients are available as well as unaltered. Furthermore, it is the only turmeric supplement available fortified with cannabinoid- and terpene-rich cannabis extract.

For transparency, the ingredients of these supplements are as follows:

Turmeric-PLUS as 500 mg gelcaps:
- wild organic ethanol-extracted turmeric resin high in curcuminoids
- wild turmeric CO_2 supercritical extract high in turmerones
- wild organic rosemary oil
- wild organic oregano oil
- organic ginger oleoresin, alcohol-extracted
- extra virgin olive oil
- beeswax
- sunflower lecithin

Canacurmin as 500 mg gelcaps:
- raw, organic hemp/cannabis stalk extract, supercritically extracted without solvents
- wild organic ethanol-extracted turmeric resin high in curcuminoids
- wild turmeric CO_2 supercritical extract high in turmerones
- wild organic rosemary oil
- wild organic oregano oil
- organic ginger oleoresin, alcohol-extracted
- extra virgin olive oil plus cold-pressed sesame oil
- beeswax
- sunflower lecithin

It can be seen that the only difference between the two is the addition of cannabis stalk extract and sesame oil in the latter. This may lead to confusion by the reader regarding, "Which should I take?" In fact, people who are in desperate need can take both formulas. Those on a budget may choose to take a formula with both active ingredients, therefore, Canacurmin. Still others may wish to avoid the intake of anything cannabis. Thus, Turmeric-PLUS is the ideal choice. As well, people who are strictly taking turmeric supplements may wish to choose this supplement if for no other reason than to replace their current one with a complex which is more potent and effective.

Solvent residues, anyone?

Fortunately, the majority of well-established turmeric supplements use ethanol, that is alcohol, as the primary solvent. This is, at least, what is said verbally and on company literature. Not all these purveyors are entirely transparent. In many instances certain petrochemicals are also applied, for instance, acetone as a wash. A carcinogen, this is the same chemical found in fingernail polish remover. Ask the manufacturer for a spec sheet or other information regarding solvents used. Of note, all curcumin isolates are solvent extracted. There is no other means to concentrate it. The issue is when using petrochemical agents, like acetone, residues always remain; any amount is unfit for human consumption.

Even worse are residues of dichloroethane, also known as EDC. There is, apparently, widespread contamination with this chemical in curcumin raw materials. According to the Toxic Substances and Disease Registry, Department of Health and

Human Services, this is a Class-1 drug, residues of which are considered toxic. Ingested levels above 5 parts per million may lead to damage of the liver, kidneys, lungs, and spleen, along with in some cases heart failure. There is also considerable neurotoxicity at this level. Long-term consumption may lead to cancer. This toxicity is so widespread that "according to the researchers curcumin extract with an EDC amount less than 5 ppm is not easily found."

This is an ominous conclusion. While, officially, the use of this solvent is discouraged, it would appear that, secretly, it is being utilized far more often than is realized. Chlorinated hydrocarbons are unfit for human consumption to any degree. Moreover, the level of corruption they cause to the chemistry of the plant matter in question is surely extreme. Then, too, there is the environmental damage. EDC and similar petrochemical solvents must be burned off. There is, therefore, significant air pollution as a consequence. Plus, with any leakage or spillage there is additional noxious pollution of the environment. After all, it's a hazardous waste and must be properly handled and disposed. What happens to the residues, then, after the extraction procedures are completed? Surely, this is problematic for all involved: the companies, its workers, and, of course, the surrounding environment. As a matter of principle and also for personal protection avoid EDC-extracted spices and/or herbs as you would avoid the plague.

Whole food turmeric revisited

The whole food form, the type used traditionally, is in many ways just as unique as supplemental concentrates. This type of turmeric is commonly produced in Pakistan, India, and Sri Lanka, the latter formerly known as Ceylon.

Here is how it is traditionally produced. The rhizomes are picked either from farms or in the wild. Before it can be used as a common food it must be processed. Typically, it is steamed or boiled to remove the rawness of the odor and also to gelatinize the starch. Traditionally, the rhizomes are placed in water-filled shallow pans or earthenware, then heated for about an hour, depending on the variety. They are removed from the water and sun-dried. When dry, they are polished to remove the rough skin. Finally, they are powdered.

In some areas of India a bizarre substance is used for the polishing: lead chromate. Residues of this chemical are deposited in the final product, which has recently caused a scandal, where common turmeric powders have shown high lead levels. This is why it is crucial when purchasing and consuming turmeric powder to use only organic sources, ideally, those which are certified. In this regard because of the use of lead chromate for heavy powder consumers it is possible to suffer chronic lead poisoning. The issue is sufficiently serious that it led to a recall. In 2016 the FDA removed multiple brands from the market because of lead contamination.

India is by far the largest producer of turmeric powder, this coming in a wide range of varieties and qualities. Even so, the first quality is the wild-growing type, followed by certified organic. Wild turmeric is found both in India and Sri Lanka. In Sri Lanka it is traditional to grow the spice in family gardens, where it virtually becomes wild. No chemicals are used. In fact, now, certified organic turmeric powders from this region are available.

Analyses have been made on such Sri Lanka turmeric powder. While the typical type has curcumin levels ranging from .3% to a maximum of 3.5% the wild-type Sri Lankan turmeric scores as high as 6%. The wild Indian type scores up to 6% or slightly higher. Thus, powders made from wild-growing turmeric are the densest in active ingredients known. Moreover, it is a whole food complex, which is only produced in the most natural, traditional means possible. The roots are dried and then pulverized. Some of the essential oils are lost via this process, but the full compliment of curcuminoids remains. Nevertheless, it remains a highly fragrant turmeric powder with a powerful, intense taste. Lead chromate is never used in the high-grade, wild and/or certified organic varieties. Additionally, there are a number of organic and/or wild Indian turmeric powders which are also free of lead and other noxious chemicals. For those who consume turmeric powder on a daily or routine basis the use of organic and/or lead-free turmeric is mandatory.

There are similar traditional spices in India and Sri Lanka that are grown in a natural, chemical-free means. These spices include ginger, black pepper, and cinnamon. The cinnamon from Sri Lanka is the original, true species, ideal for human use. It is far superior to the commercial spice, which is typically not cinnamon at all but is, rather, from the cassia genus. Cassia-type plants have a degree of toxicity, though modest, mostly in the form of gastric and/or intestinal irritation, while the Sri Lankan species is non-toxic. Thus, it can be consumed in large quantities on a regular basis. To procure such high-grade wild-organic spices, which are certified organic and/or wild, see www.americanwildfoods.com.

Absorption revisited: nanotechnology and more

It has been stated that, once isolated, the absorption of curcumin is exceedingly poor. The elements within the spice that facilitate ready utilization are lost. For curcumin this is largely because it is so insoluble in water and also because it is metabolized so rapidly. Significant blood levels simply don't occur unless it is taken at high doses, which was demonstrated in both animal and human trials. Up to 12 grams per day of curcumin were necessary to achieve significant blood levels. Of note, usually it is being consumed in *milligram* doses. This is equivalent to some 25 to 40 500 mg capsules of curcumin isolate depending on the formula. No one would consume such a dosage. This is why companies have resorted to all sorts of artifices in order to manipulate absorption. One such artifice is nanotechnlogy.

Can anyone image the degree of manipulation that is occurring? This natural complex, turmeric spice, is being corrupted with nanotechnology. What could be more bizarre than this? There is, now, incredibly, "polymer nanoparticle encapsulated" curcumin. Known as "nanocurcumin" it is supposedly "readily dispersed" into watery mediums, or at least so the marketing jargon states. This is through a most suspect process, which is to "coat" curcumin isolate with what is known as a "hydrophilic polymer." This polymer consists of particles of N-isopropylacrylamide combined with N-vinyl-2-pyrolidonne plus ethylene glycol. Of note, ethylene glycol is antifreeze, which is highly toxic. Nor is vinyl pyrolidonne considered safe for human consumption. Then, too, there is acrylamide. Who would normally ingest such a polymer? No one in their right mind would consume a natural-source substance tainted with such synthetic additives.

There are other nanoparticles which are employed in its manufacture. These substances include curcumin nanocrystals, nanoparticulates, nanoemulsions, corn dextrin-based "self-assemblies," nanosuspensions, and nanoliposomes as well as micro-gold-particle-based nanosolids. Regarding this metal-based element in addition to gold, oxides of copper, iron, zinc, aluminum, and silver are also used. Incredibly, oxides of such metals are among the most noxious metallic substances known and are wholly foreign to the body. Yet another element commonly used is titanium, which has known toxic actions upon the liver, kidneys, spleen, and heart. However, the most toxic of all according to an investigation by *Particle and Fibre Toxicology* are copper and zinc oxides.

In addition to the metallic components, which can never be healthy, there are those derived from synthetic chemicals, for instance, the lipid elements. These elements are derived from soy, which is GMO-tainted. As noted in the *International Journal of Nanomedicine* a host of other substances are used, including albumin from human or animal blood as well as gelatin, either from pork or beef. This surely poses an issue for people of certain faiths as well as vegans and vegetarians. All such components are common contaminants in nanotech-based dietary supplements. Moreover, it is an entirely experimental science with unpredictable consequences.

Mycellization: the absorption issue resolved?

Far safer in regard to dietary supplements is the use of mycellization. While nanotechnology is experimental mycels are a well-published means for facilitating absorption. In fact, mycellization is held as a generally regarding as safe (GRAS) process, that is it is non-toxic. It is a natural process which happens in the intestines with fat. In nature the mycellizing agent is bile, which fully emulsifies the fat, so it can be absorbed. Another mycellization agent is lecithin, although the only 'safe' lecithin, today, is sunflower-source. This is because the other option, soy lecithin, is GMO-tainted.

In contrast, nanotechnology is an unknown methodology, fully untested, with difficult-to-determine degrees of toxicity. Manipulation of herbs and herbal molecules with nanotech agents is categorically unnatural. For instance, how can surrounding curcumin with nanoparticles of gold, silver, or aluminum be deemed anything other than corrupt. In contrast, a mycel is, essentially, an emulsion of a fat molecule. The purpose is to render it soluble in fat. This is precisely what happens when dish soap is added to fat residues. It is also what happens when bile is secreted into the intestines or when fat is absorbed into the lymph. This is the simplest, most effective way to render fat absorbable into water mediums such as the blood and lymph.

There is a mycellized version of turmeric extract available. Known as Mycellized Turmeric-PLUS it is in a water-miscible suspension. This means that it absorbs directly into the bloodstream as well as the lymph. It can be taken, ideally, as sublingual drops and also orally in juice/water. Like its capsule version it is a combination of wild turmeric extract, rich in curcuminoids and turmerones, along with wild oils of oregano and rosemary. It also contains organic-source ginger oleoresin. This is a highly potent remedy and is aggressive as a natural antiinflammatory agent. It may be added as a 'spiking agent' to turmeric milk. It may also be added to stir-fry and/or marinades.

Synthetic versions

There are a number of synthesized versions of curcumin, which are available. These versions include tetrahydrocurcumin, its benzoic acid-based methyl ester, metal chelates of synthetic curcuminoids, and aromatic enone and dienone analogues. None of these chemicals are found in nature. The absorption of such synthetic versions is notoriously poor, while their safety is not established. Regardless, by no means should synthetic versions be consumed, as they are tainted with a number of noxious chemical derivatives, which may cause damage to the liver and kidneys. Regardless, it makes no sense to consume them, as only natural-source curcumin has been proven by laboratory tests to be effective.

Turmeric can replace drugs

In what is an obvious epidemic there are a number of pain-killing drugs to which people become addicted or at least dependent. These drugs include the following:

* opiates
* NSAIDS
* aspirin
* acetaminophen
* cortisone
* Prednisone
* SSRIs

The good news is that all such drugs can be replaced through turmeric therapy. This is true for the whole food form, the actual raw root and/or its juice as well as the truly unprocessed whole food supplement forms. It is also true of ginger, particularly high-potency ginger oleoresin as well as organic, minimally processed ginger powder. As well, the fresh root and its juice are highly effective in drug withdrawal, particularly in regard to pain-killers and antiinflammatory agents. Other herbal medicines which assist this process include organic, raw, supercritically extracted cannabis and also oil of wild oregano. Each of these natural medicines has its own novel mechanism of action for reversing pain and also for aiding in drug withdrawal. The most potent of these for assisting drug withdrawal syndromes is the raw, organic cannabis extract, known as Hempanol, the SuperStrength variety being preferred.

Another effective drug withdrawal complex is known as Oregulin. Consisting of extracted oils of myrtle, fenugreek, cumin, cinnamon, and oregano this oil is a potent one for controlling blood sugar, which is essential in any drug detoxification plan. Once again, the best results are through sublingual administration. Thus, the three most potent anti-withdrawal supplemental complexes are as follows: Tumeric-PLUS, Hempanol SuperStrength, and Oregulin sublingual drops.

Regarding turmeric, a multi-phasic approach should be taken. To withdraw from the drugs and eliminate them the turmeric extract should be taken both as capsules and sublingual drops. The spice should be consumed regularly, for instance, as turmeric milk; raw roots of ginger and turmeric should also be consumed. It can also be consumed as a complex with raw, organic cannabis stalk extract, known as Canacurmin, available both in sublingual drops and 500 mg gelcaps. For extreme cases of pain and inflammation this can be taken with the Turmeric-PLUS supplements.

Chapter Five

Wild Versus Farm-Raised

The novel powers of wild plants have been repeatedly demonstrated, both through traditional use and scientific research. This is no less true in regard to turmeric. In India, as well as Sri Lanka, a number of wild turmeric species proliferate. This is also true in the Indian National Forests and in other similar regions distant from the agri-farming locales. While it is little realized the common species, *Curcuma longa*, grows wild. The wild version has a denser amount of active ingredients than the farm-raised types. It is even richer in these active substances than organically grown plants. Investigators have discovered that the wild roots contain up to 20% more curcumin than farm-raised varieties and up to twice the content of aromatic oils, a difference which is highly significant.

It has also been discovered that wild turmeric is richer in flavor and aroma than the farm-raised types, including organic, which is no surprise considering its nature. It grows in wilderness regions among other wild plants. Thus, it is a tough, hardy plant, rich in active ingredients and taste. In all cases it is superior to harvest and utilize wild plants as medicines whenever possible. These plants have the divine imprint upon them, offering a power and potency not possible for their farmed-raised alternatives. Yet, even so, in all cases such wild-source plants must be picked ethically to avoid over-harvesting.

Why is the wild type preferable? This is related to its 'fighting for life' issue, where it must exist on its own against the elements, without being coddled and farmed. By nature, such wild-type turmerics boast a higher oil content, made for their own defense: against climactic stress, predators, insects, and more. The plant is, overall, tougher and more robust, with a thicker, larger root system, with also a greater resistance to disease. It is the potency that is optimal for the vigorous, effective treatment and reversal of disease.

Wild turmeric flourishes in regions of lesser human activity: near remote areas and forests. A hardy plant it grows often over a long period of time in relatively undisturbed soil. Here, it can develop a large rhizome, far bigger and more dense than farm-raised cousins. That dense root system can be ethically harvested, where a portion of the rhizomes remain, so it can re-grow. In such wild rhizomes are powerful phytochemicals, including a number not found in commercial types.

It tends to thrive in the wild, where it feeds off of humic acid-rich soil. Moreover, it is not only just in India where it flourishes but also can be found disseminated in the forests throughout the rest of Southeast Asia as well as in China. While the commercial type has about 4% essential oils, wild turmeric of the longa species can be as high as 8%. It is the essential oils which aid in the absorption of the tough-to-utilize active ingredient curcumin. This is why extract of wild turmeric is significantly more bioavailable than those made from farm-raised rhizomes.

It is not merely the absorption or the higher density of essential oils alone which explains this. It is true that the wild types have a higher amount of curcumin as well. Once again, it is more than this. There is a mystery regarding it. This has to do with the refined balance of nature, subtle as it is. It is a divine energy, a wholesomeness of sorts, a completeness, one which never can be duplicated by human manipulated versions. The turmeric used in the highly potent dietary supplement, Turmeric-Plus, is exclusively wild. This is true of the sublingual drops and also the 500 mg capsules. This wild-type is also found in the combination capsules, the cannabis plus turmeric extract, known as Canacurmin. The wild version of *Curcuma longa* has a multitude of uses, which complement those of its sister species. These uses in human ailments include the following:

- for the reduction of excessively high cholesterol levels
- in the treatment of gout
- for the reversal of some of the elements of diabetes
- for maintaining cardiovascular health and in the prevention of blood clots
- to reduce excessive stickiness of the platelets
- to boost bone marrow synthesis of red and white blood cells
- to bolster overall immunity
- as a powerful anticancer agent
- as a potent, systemic antiinflammatory agent
- as a means to block oxidative damage in the body
- to improve bile synthesis
- as an aid to digestion as well as stomach acid secretion
- as a means for reducing inflammation of the skin as seen

in eczema and psoriasis
• for boosting the localized immune system of the intestinal canal and therefore blocking allergic tendencies

Turmeric extract from exclusively wild-growing species of *Curcuma longa* is now available. Known as Turmeric-PLUS it is available as 500 mg gelcaps and also mycellized sublingual drops. A highly aromatic complex this supplement has a powerful turmeric odor and taste, demonstrating its pure, potent nature. It is unusual and original, since it is partly raw, the whole food fraction being extracted via supercritical or CO_2 extraction. The pigment complex, or oleoresin, is concentrated through ethanol. It is unique in the industry, however, since only certified organic ethanol is used. Moreover, absolutely no petrochemicals are utilized, as is certified by the maker. This demonstrates the care and concern of the manufacturer, North American Herb & Spice, for the end user.

Regarding wild turmeric one other notable example is *Curcuma aromatica.* Long used as a traditional herbal drug it grows wild throughout India and other parts of southeast Asia, although it is also cultivated. Over the centuries this species, among others, have been used extensively, therapeutically as well as cosmetically. *Curcuma aromatica* is also known in India as wild turmeric or musk turmeric. In contrast to *Curcuma longa*, which has pigments in the highest density, the greatest proportion of its active ingredients are volatile oils. In fact, the reason it is known as the "musk" type is because of its rich content of musk oil-like compounds, camphor and camphene. That's also why it is called "aromatica."

As will be demonstrated, here, the other essential oil components in the aromatic plant include pinene, limonene, geramcrone, curcumene, curzerenone, and borneol. In contrast, the essential oil components of the standard species are as follows:

- turmerones
- curlone
- caryophyllene
- eucalyptol (also known as 1,8 cineol or limonene)
- alpha phellandrene

Of these, the turmerones account for some 44% of the total. Then, clearly, the wild-source is an essential oil powerhouse.

This does not mean that it necessarily supercedes *Curcuma longa*, since its wild species are also potent. Rather, these natural medicines complement each other, the aromatica species, for instance, having extensive use as a medicinal cosmetic. Furthermore, whether topically or internally, it is known to exhibit significant antiinflammatory actions, antitumor capacity, cancer preventive powers, the capacity to induce wound healing, and anti-nephrotoxic activity. Note Indian investigators publishing in the *Journal of Pharmacognosy and Phytochemistry* it also is useful as a cough suppressant and acts as a modest blood thinner, preventing excessive platelet stickiness. It also has a history, they note, as an 'anti-melanin' agent, that is it has the capacity to reverse excessive melanin pigment deposits, as occurs in freckles, moles, and melanoma. Other novel uses include the reversal of corns and also the elimination of bruising.

In China, where it also grows, it was/is used traditionally as an antidote for poisonous bites, including snake bites, as well as topically for skin diseases. The Chinese also use it for excessively thick blood. Additionally, it is known in both China and India to aid complexion.

As mentioned previously *Curcuma aromatica* is significantly richer in volatile oils than other species, with a density of up to 8%. It also contains rich amounts of camphene and camphor, lacking in its farm-raised cousins. This demonstrates the need to review the active ingredients of this complex, listed as follows:

- alpha curcumene
- beta curcumene
- d-camphor
- camphene
- p-methoxycinnamic acid
- germcrene
- D curzerene
- germacrone
- alpha turmerone
- beta turmerone
- d-camphene
- p-methoxycinnamic acid
- alpha and beta pinenes
- borneol
- alpha terpeniol
- myrcene
- terpinolene
- gamma-terpinene
- limonene
- beta thujone
- alpha-copaene
- alpha-bergamotene
- beta bisabolene

- cuminic aldehyde
- cuminyl alcohol
- curcuphenol
- zingiberene
- zanthorrhizol
- curcuphenol
- beta elemene
- isolborneol
- linalool
- beta farnesene

Of note, major components include curdione, neocurdione, and germacrone. What does this complex of novel biological compounds offer? In fact, it offers a wide-ranging power for the reversal of disease syndromes. There is a particularly astonishing action in relation to brain cancer. Germacrone, a highly biologically active component of wild turmeric oil, aggressively destroys brain cancer cells, in this case versus gliomas. The oil also shuts down liver cancer cell proliferation. It also has a rather strong action against hyperpigmentation of the skin, thus blocking melanoma growth. So, it is a good medicinal adjunct to *Curcuma longa* therapy.

The essential oils are more potent as natural medicines than the pigments, like curcumin. Plus, they are more readily absorbed. Turmeric essential oils are aggressive agents against colon and breast cancer, while also helping reverse serious neurological disorders such as Alzheimer's disease, Parkinson's disease, and multiple sclerosis.

It is not merely this. In fact, the drug companies are salivating at the thought of its immense and diverse powers. Notes A. Kuttiyil, it is a "promising candidate for the development and designing of modern drugs for several diseases." Can anyone fathom it, that is it is so utilitarian that by itself it can treat a number of diseases? No synthetic drug could possibly compare to such powers.

One unique element in wild turmeric, whether the longa or aromatica species, is higher amounts of the polysaccharides. The particular compounds are known as polyxyloses. These components are antiproliferative, that is they are effective antitumor agents. In an investigation published in *Pharmacology and Biology*, 2010, these polysaccharides were evaluated. It was found inflammatory cell proliferation was reduced by some 92%, a highly significant result.

The list for which this species of turmeric is used is extensive. This list includes:

- to promote improved circulation
- to reverse hiccough
- in the treatment of bronchitis and dry cough
- for reversing yeast infections of the skin, tongue, and vaginal tract
- for speeding the healing of wounds
- as an anticancer agent
- as an antiinflammatory agent
- to combat excessive platelet levels and activity
- to block oxidative damage in the body
- as an antidiabetic agent
- to improve gallbladder function and purge gallstones
- for the prevention of coronary artery disease
- to block and reverse excessive growth of blood vessels, as is seen in active tumors
- to kill and purge worms
- to ease and prevent cardiac arrhythmia

These actions are far more diverse and extensive than those of isolate-based turmeric extracts from commercially raised root such as BCM-95 and its likes.

Versus farm-raised ones wild extracts are particularly effective against colon and liver cancer. They are also the most potent type for reversing melanoma and various other skin diseases.

The aromatica species has definite value as a natural medicine. It is more bitter than the longa species. Even so, it has a utility which complements the powers of its more well-known cousin. There are a few precautions with this type, as it should not be given in large quantities to conceiving, pregnant, and/or nursing mothers. This is not true of the wild version of the longa species, which can be used with impunity. Hopefully, a *Curcuma aromatica* supplement will soon become available.

Wild versus organic

There is a considerable difference in wild plants versus farm-raised. This is even true of those which are organically produced. It has, for instance, now been proven that the wild-growing turmeric is superior to organic, even if it is certified. While pesticides and herbicides are not an issue with organic, they are also never a concern with wild plants. The challenge with organic is that it is specifically grown. This means that it is under farming controls. This weakens the plant, causing it to produce a more diminished degree of active ingredients.

This is now demonstrated through extraction results. Wild turmeric has up to 25% higher densities of active ingredients than certified organic, including much higher amounts of the all-important polyphenol, curcumin. There is also the issue of pathogen contamination or overload. The amount of potentially dangerous germs in the commercially raised types and even organically raised roots is exceedingly high. Levels of pathogens can be up to 100,000 per count or even more. Such levels are not seen in properly harvested and processed wild roots and their derivatives. With the powder produced by North American Herb & Spice (NAHS) germ levels are below 5000 per unit count, which is well below the acceptable amount. Moreover, NAHS uses a special kind of process, which virtually sterilizes the root and its powder without the use of the traditional methods of boiling and dry, oven-style heat.

With the more gentle processing there is another great advantage over both commercial and organic options. This is in regard to the levels in the powder of that group of active ingredients, the turmerones. The NAHS-produced powder contains turmerone levels of up to 1.25%, which is incredibly high. All others are .2% or less, a 10-fold reduction. So, no doubt, wild is superior, and this is why it is exclusively used in both the various turmeric powders, food complexes, and also in the mycellized and gelcap supplements. The latter also have certified organic additions in the form of curcumin-rich resins.

Chapter Six

Inflammatory Diseases

It should be kept in mind that, historically, turmeric was most well known as a treatment for pain and inflammation. In antiquity there were no pill forms with only the whole, unprocessed root and the carefully processed, dried root powder being available. Extracts were occasionally made but nothing like those produced today. Thus, as proven by history it is not necessary to consume a highly processed and industrially manipulated supplement to gain the benefits of this spice.

Supplements, though, can be available, particularly when they act as concentrates of wholesome active ingredients. The ideal approach, then, is to use all three:

- the fresh, whole (ideally organically-raised) root
- a high-grade form of the whole spice, also ideally organically raised and non-irradiated
- a top quality, non-petrochemical solvent extracted root complex containing both curcumin and the full compliment of the essential oils, including the turmerones as well as the other wholesome, naturally occurring elements of the unprocessed spice

There is sound reason for this. All the key active ingredients of turmeric, including the pigments and essential oils, are antiinflammatory. Curcumin can inhibit both the activity and the synthesis of cyclooxygenase-2 (COX2) and 5-lipoxygenase (5-LOX) as well as a host of other enzymes which induce inflammation. For instance, studies have determined that the various curcuminoids, when taken together, blocked inflammatory pathways, preventing the production of a protein which triggers pain and swelling. As demonstrated by investigators publishing in *Clinical Nutrition*, even common protein markers in the blood stream, like C-reactive protein or CRP, are positively affected, with in one human study all consumers of curcumin having lower levels. There was a bonus, which was an antidiabetic affect, with lower blood glucose and hemoglobin A1c levels. This benefit was also likely a result of its antiinflammatory actions. The placebo group had, in contrast, no improvement in blood sugar levels or inflammation. Essentially, this means that this turmeric active ingredient is effective in reversing the toxicity and inflammatory consequences of metabolic syndrome, allowing insulin to not only be less noxious but also more well utilized. This caused the investigators to recommend turmeric and/or its extracts for anyone with a high CRP level.

There are other markers of inflammation that are blocked. A rather comprehensive list, as published by N. Chainai-Wu in the *Journal of Alternative and Complimentary Medicine*, is as follows:

- inhibition of cyclooxygenase (COX-2)
- blockage of lipooxygenase

- inhibition of phospholipase and thromboxane
- blockage of the activity of prostaglandins in general
- reduction of nitric oxide
- inhibition of collagenase and elastase
- blockage of monocyte chemoattractant protein
- reduction of interferon-inducible protein
- blockade of tumor necrosis factor
- reduction of interleukin-12

The ability of turmeric and its extracts, in the case of above, curcumin, to stabilize the body and cause such an improvement in physiology is two-fold. It is a consequence of its inflammation-blocking powers as well as its antioxidant capacities. The same is true for a host of other spices, including wild rosemary and oregano. Regarding wild oregano it offers another mechanism of action, which is an aggressive antiseptic power. By killing noxious, invasive germs in all cases inflammation and oxidative damage are eased. In fact, in some cases the inflammation is caused solely by the infection alone. This is why purging the infection can be more instrumental for achieving the cure than taking antiinflammatory agents.

In all such protocols a number of therapeutic agents are described. This is to give people the full compliment of options. This is necessary, because many of the mentioned disease syndromes are extreme and heavy intervention is necessary to resolve them. As a rule, though, there are three powerful antiinflammatory agents which are universal in their powers and scope. These potent agents are turmeric and its various extracts, wild oregano, wild rosemary, and cannabis. For those on a budgetary concern there is one supplement that contains all three of these natural medicines. Known as Canacurmin if there would be only one formula to try this would be the option. It is a combination of the following:

- supercritical whole food and raw wild turmeric extract
- supercritical and raw organic cannabis extract
- CO2 organic ginger extract
- wild rosemary oil
- wild oregano oil

Organic, whole food cannabis extract can also be found on its own, complexed with supercritical oregano. Known as Hempanol it is rich in the highly antinflammatory terpene, Beta Caryophyllene. It is an excellent adjunct, along with turmeric extracts and whole food turmeric powder, in the treatment of inflammatory disorders.

Arthritis

In traditional Chinese and Indian Ayurveda medicine, turmeric is used to treat this condition. A 2006 study found that turmeric helps reduce joint inflammation. A different study from the same year found it to have significant anti-arthritic effects. There is even evidence, as demonstrated by an investigation in 2012, that curcumin might even be more effective for rheumatoid arthritis than anti-inflammatory drugs.

There can be no question about the powers of turmeric and its extracts versus this disease. The research is highly definitive. Consider the work of Indian investigators, Amand and his group, on arthritis of the knee. Here, it was found that extract of Indian turmeric was equal in pain reliving powers to ibuprofen, that is Motrin. Some people are dependent upon this class of drugs, Advil, Motrin, and the like, for daily survival. They could become 'dependant' instead on extracts of turmerics: without risk of side effects.

A rather novel study was conducted by J.L. Funk and her group. Published in *Arthritis & Rheumatology* the results demonstrated that turmeric extract blocked the expression of genes which mediate joint inflammation and infection. The influx of inflammatory cells within the joints was greatly reduced, a major consequence. Joint levels of inflammatory prostaglandins, notably of the E series, were also suppressed. In addition, there was a direct effect versus the osteoclasts, those bone- and joint tissue-eating cells, which, too, were inhibited. In yet another investigation in rheumatoid arthritis patients published by *Phytotherapy Research*, 2012, turmeric extract was matched to the drug diclofenac sodium to see which was most effective. The turmeric or, rather, curcumin group did best, suffering less pain than the drug group and also having an increased range of movement. Plus, unlike the drug, the curcumin users suffered no side effects.

Turmeric's powers against this condition are greatly facilitated by other highly antiinflammatory spice components, notably extracts of wild rosemary, wild oregano, and ginger. Ideally, all these spice extracts should be taken together to maximize the antiinflammatory and immune modulation response as well as to aid most aggressively in reversing any arthritic lesions.

Treatment protocol

- whole food, mycellized wild turmeric extract with wild rosemary, wild oregano, and raw ginger extract: 20 drops two or three times daily

- whole food wild turmeric complex as 500 mg gelcaps:

two or more gelcaps two or three times daily

- whole food, organic turmeric powder: two tsp. twice daily

- raw, organic turmeric: at least one root daily; take in turmeric milk or add to recipes

- bone activating capsules with wild oregano, rosemary, and sage plus raw bone from New Zealand grass-fed cattle: two or more capsules twice daily

- bone activating rubbing oil as a topical anti-pain and antiinflammatory rub: apply topically as needed

- raw whole food cannabis extract with supercritical raw turmeric plus oregano and rosemary oils as sublingual drops: 20 or more drops twice daily or as gelcaps, two or more twice daily

Rheumatoid arthritis

In this condition there is an even more extreme degree of inflammation and pain than in osteoarthritis. This is the type that leads to great deformation of the joints, including gross disfigurement.

In all cases rheumatoid arthritis is associated with infection. It is the infectious agents which cause the joint destruction, the inflammation being secondary. Thus, while turmeric is a key element in the treatment so is that powerful antiseptic spice extract, oil of wild oregano.

In one study by J.L. Funk of the University of Arizona College of Medicine curcuminoid concentrate, made in the lab from whole turmeric roots, demonstrated a definite anti-arthritic action against experimental rheumatoid arthritis in the animal model. Essentially, the curcuminoid complex prevented the onset of the disease. The conclusion was that this natural medicine inhibits a DNA transcription factor, NF-KB, from being activated within the joints. This, the investigators noted, is the same mechanism of action for anti-arthritic pharmaceutical drugs. Moreover, by blocking the inflammatory process inside of the joints, consequently, the joint tissues are able to heal. Even so, the wild oregano oil can also be used, rubbed over the joint and also taken internally, to purge all infestation.

Treatment protocol

- whole food, wild turmeric extract with naturally occurring curcuminoids and turmerones plus wild rosemary and oregano: two 500 mg capsules twice daily

- whole food, mycellized wild turmeric extract with wild rosemary, wild oregano, and raw ginger extract: 20 or more drops two three times daily

- bone activating rubbing oil: rub on rheumatic lesions as often as desired; also, take 10 or more drops under the tongue, as needed

- Super-Strength oil of wild oregano: take five or more drops twice daily, also use topically, as needed; wild oregano oil has morphine-like properties

- raw whole food cannabis extract with supercritical raw turmeric plus oregano and rosemary oils as sublingual drops: 20 or more drops twice daily or as gelcaps, two or more twice daily

Lyme disease

In Lyme disease turmeric plays a significant role. This is largely because of its antiinflammatory properties and also its capacity to reverse nerve cell damage. Lyme is associated with much neurological damage. Turmeric helps repair this, acting directly on the nerve centers, even aiding in the regeneration of diseased or damaged brain cells. It is also invaluable in blocking the Lyme-induced inflammatory toxicity within the joints. Turmeric works best in combating Lyme when combined with wild oregano-based supplements, the latter acting as germicidal purges against the Lyme bacillus as well as the various co-infection agents. This is a most treacherous disease process. It involves an attack upon the body by that cork-screw pathogen, the spirochete *Borellia burgdorferi.* This germ readily invades the body, with a predilection for the skin, cartilage-joint lining, heart, spinal cord, and brain. Infection by this spirochete is usually complicated by the so-called co-infections, including infestation by the bacterial agents bartonella and ehrlichia and the protozoan, babesia. Other noxious agents include tick-borne viruses and the highly immunosuppressive pseudo-bacteria, mycoplasma.

Wild rosemary and sage are also effective anti-Lyme adjuncts, particularly their extracted essential oils. A combination of these oils with wild oregano oil, known a BoneACTIV rubbing oil, is an essential therapeutic complex for Lyme disease reversal. This oil is potent as a remedy rubbed topically on any painful joint and also as sublingual drops. Ginger is yet another spice complex that is anti-Lyme. Both the fresh root and raw CO_2 extract, as well as the oleoresin, are effective remedies. The antiinflammatory enzymes bromelain and papain are ideal additions to the therapeutic regimen, as these act as powerful agents for combating deep-seated inflammation within the joints, muscles, and nerve centers. A combination of these enzymes, along with turmeric and ginger, is available as Inflam-EEZ capsules, which can be added to the anti-Lyme protocol.

To eradicate Lyme the wild oregano must be taken aggressively. To do so it is essential to use that daily use, edible type: P73 Oreganol. This can be used in massive quantities, like 40 to 80 drops three or four times daily. It is most effective when combined with the multiple spice complex consisting of dried oils of wild oregano, sage, and cumin, along with dried cinnamon oil. The juice or essence of wild oregano may be invaluable for driving the germ out of the central nervous system and, thus, reversing neurological Lyme.

In all Lyme cases there is a significant challenge to achieve the full cure. It can be done, but it takes persistence and much time. The spirochete is difficult to eradicate. It may take up to six months to fully purge it, in some cases even longer. For a variety of protocols for natural medicines, depending upon the severity, see *The Lyme Disease Cure*, same author, Knowledge House Publishers (www.cassingram.com).

Treatment protocol

- whole food turmeric extract with wild rosemary, wild oregano, and raw ginger extract: 40 drops three times daily or two gelcaps two or three times daily

- whole food, organic turmeric powder: two tsp. twice daily

- raw, organic turmeric: at least one root daily

- juice or essence of wild oregano: a half ounce twice daily

- antiinflammatory bromelain-papain complex with organic turmeric and ginger: three or more capsules twice daily on an empty stomach

- Beta-caryophyllene-rich raw whole food cannabis extract with supercritical wild oregano: 20 or more drops twice daily or as gelcaps, two or more twice daily

- bone- and joint-activating rubbing oil for internal and topical use: rub vigorously over any involved area, and take 20 or more drops twice daily

- raw CO$_2$-extracted organic cannabis stalk extract plus raw CO$_2$ turmeric: one or two capsules twice daily, while also taking the sublingual drops, 20 or more drops twice daily

Gout

Traditionally, turmeric is used in the treatment of this condition. Gout is associated with the accumulation of uric acid in the tissues, which then deposits in the joints as urate crystals. Such crystals cause a great degree of pain and inflammation, leading to gout attacks.

The enzyme which agitates this, xanthine oxidase, is blocked by turmeric. It is essentially the same mechanism offered by the anti-gout drug, allopurinol. In a Chinese study done in 2009 curcumin was found to block the enzyme to such a degree that it caused an obvious reduction in chronic inflammation. Other mechanisms of its anti-gout actions were determined by Zhang and his group, where the active ingredient curcumin caused a flushing out of uric acid and its crystals through the urine. A number of studies have shown that it lowers uric acid levels in the blood, perhaps through the same mechanism. Additionally, wild oregano helps normalize uric acid levels and is highly effective as an anti-gout agent, particularly when combined with the gout-fighting herb, *Rhus coriaria*. The combination, known as OregaMax, is a powerful complex for purging excessive amounts of uric acid from the system as well as preventing the formation of the crystals. The oil of wild oregano is also a potent remedy and should be taken as a routine and also applied topically, as needed, along with turmeric extracts, including the mycellized sublingual drops.

Treatment protocol

- whole food, wild turmeric extract with wild rosemary and oregano: one or two capsules twice daily

- whole food, wild turmeric extract as sublingual drops, mycellized: 10 or more drops as often as needed

- Super-Strength oil of wild oregano: apply topically as needed and take five or more drops twice daily

- whole, crude herb wild oregano with Rhus coriaria: two or more capsules twice daily

- Beta-caryophyllene-rich raw whole food cannabis extract with supercritical wild oregano: 20 or more drops twice daily or as gelcaps, two or more twice daily

Lupus and scleroderma

As a rule lupus is an inflammatory disease, the same being true of scleroderma. Yet, they are also both infectious diseases. This is why spices and their extracts are ideal treatments. Because of its antiinflammatory powers turmeric is part of the answer for these conditions. Another crucial therapy is wild oregano oil, since this acts as a germicide to purge all pathogens, especially fungi, which are a major cause of these syndromes. An additional infectious cause is viruses, notably canine salivary virus. Thus, wild oregano extracts are a crucial therapeutic modality for reversing lupus, scleroderma, and similar connective tissue disease syndromes.

The nephritis of lupus has been shown to respond to turmeric. Yet, it also is effectively treated with wild oregano, both the oil and the whole, raw, crude herb with *Rhus coriaria.*

Scleroderma also responds positively to turmeric treatment. Both the whole food forms and the unprocessed, full complex as a supplement are effective adjuncts for reducing the inflammation of this disease. Wild oregano is also a crucial treatment modality, as it helps purge the infections associated with this condition. Of note, these infections include infestation by *Candida albicans* and also slow growing tubercular pathogens. Regarding lupus, canine salivary virus, which people contract from the saliva of dogs, is the major factor.

In particular, in scleroderma but also in lupus the Super-Strength form is much needed, rubbed topically and also taken internally as sublingual drops. As well, the aromatic essence or juice of wild oregano is an essential treatment for both these conditions.

Treatment protocol

- whole food, wild turmeric extract with wild rosemary and oregano: one or more capsules twice daily

- whole food, wild turmeric extract as sublingual drops, mycellized: 20 or more drops as often as needed

- organic turmeric powder complexed with cinnamon and ginger as turmeric milk: one or two cups daily

- Super-Strength oil of wild oregano: five or more drops twice daily, also applied topically as often as possible

- juice or essence of wild oregano (Oreganol P73 Juice): one or more ounces daily

- Beta-caryophyllene-rich raw whole food cannabis extract with supercritical wild oregano: 20 or more drops twice daily

- raw whole food cannabis extract with supercritical raw turmeric plus oregano and rosemary oils as sublingual drops: 20 or more drops twice daily or as gelcaps, two or more twice daily

Cystic fibrosis

Historically, turmeric has been used for lung diseases. It helps block mucous formation and can also aid in the expelling of mucous plugs. This makes it invaluable in cystic fibrosis, which is associated with a defect in the clearing of mucous.

There is a need for a wide range of spice medicines in this condition. Patients with this disease are vulnerable to lung infections, particularly by the opportunistic pathogen, pseudomonas. This can prove deadly, as both mucous clearance and localized immunity are compromised. Oil of wild oregano is invaluable in the treatment of this condition, since it outright destroys this pathogen, among others. Taken regularly, it also helps prevent opportunistic infections while also aiding in the breakdown and clearance of mucous plugs. The power of turmeric is greatly enhanced by the wild oregano therapy as well as, in regard to pain syndromes, the intake of cannabis-based turmeric supplements.

Treatment protocol

- whole food, wild, raw supercritical turmeric extract as sublingual drops or capsules: either ten to twenty drops under the tongue twice daily or two 500 mg gelcaps once or twice daily

- whole food, wild mycellized turmeric as sublingual drops: 20 or more drops two or more times daily

- juice or essence of wild oregano: one half ounce twice or more often daily

- oil of wild oregano, edible daily use type: 5 to 10 or more drops under the tongue multiple times daily

- multiple spice complex consisting of dessicated oils of wild oregano and sage plus cumin and cinnamon oils: two or more capsules twice daily

- Beta-caryophyllene-rich raw whole food cannabis extract with supercritical wild oregano: 20 or more drops twice daily or as gelcaps, two or three twice daily

- wild turmeric-oregano honey as an anti-mucous agent: One T. twice daily

Pulmonary fibrosis

It has been long known that turmeric is an anti-fibrotic agent. This is largely a consequence of its significant antiinflammatory actions. Other treatment modalities include wild oregano extracts and whole food, non-GMO vitamin E.

Turmeric exerts a direct action on the lungs, blocking inflammatory reactions. Once the inflammation is quelled the tissue can begin to heal. In pulmonary fibrosis there is virtually always an infectious component, with molds and other fungal invaders being the primary instigators. For the fibrosis to be halted and reversed the infection(s) must be purged. To do so it is necessary to consume the ultimate antifungal agent, oil of wild oregano, along with the aromatic juice or essence. It is also important to increase the consumption of vitamin C in a whole food form, for instance, from camu camu, rose hips, and acerola cherry; these are non-allergenic forms. If tolerated, citrus can be increased, as this is a dense source of the vitamin.

Treatment protocol

- whole food, wild turmeric extract with wild rosemary and oregano: one or two capsules twice daily

- whole food, wild turmeric extract as sublingual drops, mycellized: 10 or more drops as often as needed

- Turmeric milk made with organic turmeric and ginger: one or two cups daily

- Super-Strength oil of wild oregano: five or more drops under the tongue twice daily, or as gelcaps, one or two twice daily

- aromatic essence, that is juice of wild oregano: a half ounce twice daily

- whole food vitamin C complex from camu camu and acerola cherry: two capsules twice daily

- Beta-caryophyllene-rich raw whole food cannabis extract with supercritical wild oregano: 20 or more drops twice daily or as gelcaps, two twice daily

Sciatica

With sciatica there is great pain and inflammation in the sciatic nerve. This is usually a sign of pressure on the nerve root within the spinal cord. The pain typically radiates along the pathology of the sciatic nerve, which branches from the lower back through the hips, then, along the buttocks and down the back of the leg. It is virtually always a consequence of compression against the spinal column.

Turmeric is highly effective in the treatment of this condition. In many instances it virtually obliterates it. This is because of its powers in blocking inflammatory reactions within the nerves. Other powerful cures for sciatica include oils of wild oregano and rosemary. Such oils are conveniently found in BoneACTIV rubbing oil, which is highly effective in curbing sciatica pain both taken internally and rubbed topically. Other therapeutic agents include the antiinflammatory plant enzymes, bromelain and papain. Ginger also possesses antiinflammatory powers against this condition.

The immense therapeutic powers of turmeric-ginger extract is demonstrated by the following case history:

CASE HISTORY:

Ms. M. had suffered with sciatica for some 12 years, causing her relentless pain. Opting against surgery she attempted to treat it through conservative means: to no avail. Then, she discovered the crude, unprocessed raw turmeric extract made from wild turmeric. Taking 20 drops under the tongue twice daily the sciatica was obliterated and she is now fully pain-free.

Treatment protocol

- whole food, wild, raw supercritical turmeric extract as sublingual drops or capsules: twenty or more drops under the tongue twice daily or two 500 mg gelcaps once or twice daily

- BoneACTIV rubbing oil with oils of wild rosemary and oregano as a topical anti-pain agent: apply topically as often as needed and also take internally, 20 drops twice daily

- antiinflammatory bromelain-papain complex with organic turmeric and ginger: three or more capsules twice daily on an empty stomach

- raw CO_2-extracted organic cannabis stalk extract plus raw CO_2 turmeric: one or two capsules twice daily

- one two-inch piece of turmeric cut up or shredded and used in food

Bulging or ruptured intervertebral disc

Many people desire a non-surgical treatment for this condition. This is understandable, since the surgery leaves much to be desired and can, often, turn the individual into a cripple. One surgery begets another. The vicious cycle usually leads to rather than any improvement an increase in pain and disability. There is a wide range of spice extracts and/or concentrates that offer powers for reversing these syndromes. These include both internal and topical treatments. Additionally, there is a need for quality osteopathic therapy, which can in the case of building discs essentially reverse it. Chaga, wild oregano, wild rosemary, wild turmeric, along with ginger, bromelain, and papain, are all effective in reversing these conditions. The goal is to induce self-healing, in order to avoid surgical intervention and also to eliminate the pain. For extreme conditions the hemp/cannabis-turmeric complex is indicated, ideally as mycellized sublingual drops.

Treatment protocol

- whole food, wild, raw supercritical turmeric extract as sublingual drops or capsules: either ten to twenty drops under the tongue twice daily or two 500 mg gelcaps once or twice daily: or both

- whole food, wild mycellized turmeric as sublingual drops: 10 to 20 or more drops two or more times daily

- antiinflammatory bromelain-papain complex with organic turmeric and ginger: three or more capsules twice daily on an empty stomach

- juice of raw ginger and turmeric: an ounce twice daily in juice or water or added to turmeric milk recipe

- raw CO_2-extracted organic cannabis stalk extract plus raw CO_2 turmeric: one or two capsules twice daily

- wild, raw chaga sublingual drops and/or capsules with birch bark and wild oregano: 40 drops twice daily or with the capsules, two twice daily

- raw whole food cannabis extract with supercritical raw turmeric plus oregano and rosemary oils as sublingual drops: 20 or more drops twice daily or as gelcaps, two or more twice daily

- whole food wild turmeric powder in turmeric milk or food: two tsp. daily

Low back pain

No doubt, low back pain can be caused by disc disease. Yet, there are also a number of other factors, including muscle spasm and tension. Regardless of the cause spice-based medicines are the answer. For low back pain turmeric extracts, along with the whole food forms, is a boon. Yet, so are other spice oil components, like oil of wild oregano and oil of wild rosemary. As well, wild chaga is an effective adjunct for reversing back pain, particularly the raw forms such as the raw, wild sublingual drops and also the capsules with raw birch bark and wild oregano.

Treatment protocol

- whole food, wild, raw supercritical turmeric extract as sublingual drops or capsules: either ten to twenty drops under the tongue twice daily and/or two 500 mg gelcaps once or twice daily

- bone activating rubbing oil with wild oregano, rosemary, and sage oils: apply topically as
often as desired

- whole food complex of bromelain plus papain with turmeric and ginger: two or three capsules twice daily on an empty stomach

- raw, supecritical CO_2-extracted organic cannabis stalk extract plus raw CO_2 turmeric: one or two capsules twice daily and/or as sublingual drops, 20 or more drops twice daily

- wild, raw chaga sublingual drops and/or capsules with birch bark and wild oregano: 40 drops twice daily or with the capsules, two twice daily

Chapter Seven

Nervous System Disorders

One of the most well-established arenas for turmeric relates to disorders of the nervous system. Here, it offers a protective role in the reversal of diseases of this system. Additionally, it represents that rare capacity to induce nerve cell regeneration. This is why it is an essential component of any treatment plan for disorders of the brain, spinal cord, and peripheral nerves.

Epilepsy and seizure syndromes

Regarding seizure syndromes turmeric plays a valuable role. It is primarily the volatile oils that have the most vigorous anti-epileptic powers. In a study published in *PLoS One,* 2013, the turmeric sequiterpenes in this case ar-turmerone, was evaluated in a study of epileptic mice. It was clear from the study that the turmeric oil compound halted seizure activity, while showing no untoward effects. In fact, in any neurological condition it is the turmeric essential oil compounds that will prove to be most effective. Moreover, this oil was found to be significantly more potent than the standard type of turmeric extract available, that is curcumin. Clearly, then, for a turmeric extract to be optimally effective against epilepsy and various other seizure syndromes rich amounts of turmerones must be present.

Extract of cannabis is also highly effective for this condition. The same is true of wild oregano, particularly the steam distilled oil and also the supercritical extract. Additionally, the wild oregano aromatic essence and/or juice is a most effective remedy. So is the oil of wild oregano, particularly if taken sublingually. The oil and juice act to purge pathogens from the brain, which act as instigating agents for the development of seizures. For optimal results all such treatments should be utilized simultaneously. The crude, raw cannabis extract, combined with supercritical wild oregano, that is Hempanol, is one of the most effective anti-seizure remedies known. Incredibly, both wild oregano and cannabis have been used as anti-seizure medicines since antiquity, being particularly popular in ancient Greece.

Treatment protocol

- whole food turmeric extract with wild rosemary, wild oregano, and raw ginger extract: 40 drops three times daily or two gelcaps two or three times daily

- whole food, organic turmeric powder: two tsp. twice daily as a food/smoothie additive or in turmeric milk recipes

- raw, organic turmeric: at least one root daily

- Super-Strength oil of wild oregano: five or more drops under the tongue twice daily, or as gelcaps, one or two twice daily

- aromatic essence, that is juice of wild oregano: a half ounce twice daily

- whole food vitamin C complex from camu camu and acerola cherry: two capsules twice daily

- Beta-caryophyllene-rich raw whole food cannabis extract with supercritical wild oregano: 10 or more drops twice daily

Alzheimer's disease

There is significant proof that Alzheimer's disease, along with various other forms of dementia, respond to turmeric therapy. In fact, turmeric and its extracts exert both preventive and curative actions. Such powers have been confirmed by a plethora of animal, as well as human, studies. In rats turmeric extracts have been found to reverse dementia-associated degenerative changes in the brain; for instance, amyloid plaque formation has been reversed, proven by repeat CT-scans.

In India there is yet another proof. This relates to the overall Alzheimer's incidence. Here, this disease is virtually non-existent. The prevalence of the disease in adults aged 70 to 80 is nearly five-fold less than in Americans of the same age. Similar findings were reported in Asia, where curry consumption as little as once or twice per week is associated with an increase in cognitive powers versus non-curry eaters.

The average Indian consumes some two grams of curcumin per day, along with significant amounts of turmeric powder and/or the fresh root. Therefore, it must be the turmeric which is protective.

Researchers at UCLA decided to study this phenomenon. They found that the powerful turmeric pigment curcumin helped macrophages clear amyloid plaques found in Alzheimer's disease. Even so, the turmeric component also directly reverses amyloid pigment toxicity. Just how it does so is now known. Curcumin is highly lipid soluble and can, thus, pass through all cell membranes, particularly those of brain cells. Thus, it exerts its effects intracellularly, which is a rare action indeed. Once in the cells it interacts with the DNA, halting amyloid pigment deposition, while also causing its purging. Simultaneously, it decreases the excess proliferation of neural cells that leads to amyloid deposition.

As described by S. Mishra and K. Palanivelu in The Effect of Curcumin on Alzheimer's Disease: an Overview the spice exerts great powers within the brain to halt inflammatory processes. It blocks, they note, the enzyme cyclooxygenase or COX-2, while also inhibiting transcription factor and phospholipases, all of which facilitate Alzheimer's-related neurodegeneration. The release of noxious forms of oxygen, free radicals, is reduced, while the production of so-called pro-inflammatory cytokines is minimized.

Its antioxidant actions on the brain cannot be neglected. Turmeric pigments essentially coat the brain cells, penetrating into the most deep elements, where they absorb and detoxify noxious free radicals. Moreover, the essential oil components, the turmerones, readily penetrate the brain matter, where they, too, block oxidative damage, specifically the type that leads to neuron damage. The turmerones offer the added benefit of inducing regeneration of damaged nerve cells. Moreover, in a study done by Indian investigators curcumin was found to protect brain mitochondria from free radical-induced damage. As well, it was found to elevate brain levels of the powerful antioxidant enzyme, glutathione peroxidase.

Treatment protocol

- whole food turmeric extract with wild rosemary, wild oregano, and raw ginger extract: 40 drops three times daily or two gelcaps two or three times daily

- whole food, organic turmeric powder: two tsp. twice daily, ideally as turmeric or Golden Milk, the emulsified form for easier absorption

- raw, organic turmeric: at least one root daily

- raw, organic cannabis extract with wild, raw oregano extract: 20 drops twice daily or three gelcaps twice daily

- juice of wild oregano P73: a half ounce once or twice daily

- essence of wild rosemary for increasing mental acuity: a half ounce once or twice daily

- supercritical, raw whole food cannabis extract with supercritical wild turmeric plus wild rosemary oil: two 500 mg capsules daily

Parkinson's disease

As in Alzheimer's disease the regular and even occasional intake of turmeric or curry powder is associated with a reduced incidence. As well, evidence exists that nerve cell damage related to Parkinson's disease is reversible through turmeric therapy. In particular, the essential oil components, the turmerones, induce new cell growth while also stimulating the repair of damaged neurons.

In this disease turmeric works best when combined with wild oregano therapy. This relates to the ultimate cause of many cases of this disease, which is infestation, notably by the Lyme spirochete and various neurotropic viruses. Oil of wild oregano and the aromatic essence or juice help purge such destructive pathogens from the brain, allowing the neurological organ centers to heal.

The rigidity of Parkinson's disease is directly related to infectious damage. In fact, the disease can have as its provocation the direct injection of infectious matter, notably through vaccines. In particular, the flu vaccine, which introduces live viruses and other pathogens into the brain, may readily cause it. Tick bites, as indicated, are another primary cause, and in virtually all cases spirochete infection of the brain matter must be presumed. In the lab of Lida Mattman, Ph.D. the brains of some 80%-plus of Parkinson's disease cases were found to be infected by the Lyme spirochete. For obvious reasons edible, daily use oil of wild oregano is one of the key therapeutic interventions for treating this condition. It works most effectively when combined with the aromatic essence or juice of wild oregano as well as whole food turmeric extract.

Treatment protocol

- juice or essence of wild oregano: a half ounce or more twice daily

- oil of wild oregano, edible type, daily use: 20 or more drops three times daily

- whole food, raw turmeric extract with both curcumin and turmerones as 500 mg gelcaps: one or two capsules twice daily

- organic turmeric powder complexed with cinnamon and ginger as Turmeric milk: one or two cups daily

- mycellized wild turmeric oil with oils of wild rosemary and oregano: 10 or more drops twice daily

- neurological-supporting aromatic essence complex (that is Neuroloft): one or more ounces daily

- Ecologic 500 probiotic complex: tsp. at night in luke-warm water

- supercritical, raw whole food cannabis extract with supercritical wild turmeric plus wild rosemary oil: two 500 mg capsules daily

Note: many of these protocols in this chapter and throughout the rest of the book call for rather high doses of antiseptic spice oils, particularly the oil of wild oregano. Such high intake may result in a depletion of the healthy bacteria. Thus, it is advisable to take a probiotic daily, usually an hour or two after taking the high dose wild oregano therapy. An ideal probiotic for this purpose is the HealthBAC, which has the special property of vigorously implanting into the colon. The ideal way to take this is at night in a glass of luke-warm water, about a half teaspoon or more.

Prebiotics help feed the growth of these bacteria. Such prebiotics include raw honey, raw yacon syrup (available only under the brand name, Yac-o-Power), and arabinogalactan, the active ingredient of tamarack or larch bark. Here, then, is an ideal protocol for the building up of powerful, robust levels of probiotic, that is healthy, bacteria:

- HealthBAC vegetarian (plant-source) probiotic supplement of the formula known as Ecologic 500: a half teaspoon at night in luke-warm water

- wild tamarack bark tea (Lovely-Larch tea): a cup or two after supper

- organic, raw yacon syrup: tsp. daily

- raw honey: T. daily or, preferably, the raw, wild oregano plus wild turmeric powder mix, one or two T. daily

The raw honey can be eliminated for those who are ultra-sugar sensitive or who are diabetic. Yacon syrup is non-caloric and non-glycemic and is actually highly anti-diabetic.

Regardless of the disease process a healthy, stable gut flora is an effective means for the achievement of overall health. Such flora are necessary for healthy gut ecology, while also bolstering, as well as balancing, overall health.

Multiple sclerosis

Turmeric is a great aid for the treatment and reversal of this disease. It provides a power to give disease victims new hope, especially when combined with other spice-based natural medicines. In this condition the brain and spinal cord are infected by destructive pathogens, one of the most common of which are spirochetes, including *Borrelia burgdorferi*. Various herpetic pathogens have also been associated, as are fungal agents and chlamydia. All such invaders are readily purged by oil of wild oregano and its aromatic essence or juice.

The source of the infection may be difficult to determine. An obvious one is tick bites. However, mosquitoes also carry pathogens, which may infect the brain, including the Lyme spirochete. Additionally, dental infections may ascend into the brain, either causing the disease or aggravating it. There is another major source, which is vaccination. In fact, in some cases this is the sole source and to a large degree these septic inoculations are the cause of the MS epidemic.

In this regard the role of viruses must be considered. Whether from vaccines or other sources these pathogens readily attack the nerve sheath, stripping it of its protective coating, the myelin sheath. It is now known that a variety of herpetic viruses attack the brain in susceptible persons. For this condition to be resolved all such viruses must be purged from the body. Turmeric aids in this process, as does, in particular, edible wild oregano oil, ideally the P73 blend. Another most powerful agent is the essence of juice of wild oregano, which readily crossed the blood-brain barrier to attack and destroy noxious viral agents. Wild oregano and its essence have been shown to categorically destroy viruses, largely by dissolving their outer coating membrane.

Treatment protocol

- whole food, raw turmeric extract with both curcumin and turmerones as 500 mg gelcaps: one or two capsules twice daily

- whole food mycellized turmeric sublingual drops with wild rosemary and oregano oil: 20 drops twice daily

- juice or essence of wild oregano: a half ounce or more twice daily

- organic turmeric powder complexed with cinnamon and ginger as turmeric milk, one or two cups daily

- neurological-supporting aromatic essence complex (that is Neuroloft): one or more ounces daily

- Ecologic 500 probiotic complex: tsp. at night in luke-warm water

- whole food fatty salmon oil, rich in naturally occurring vitamins A and D (PolarPower): two or more capsules twice daily

- supercritical, raw whole food cannabis extract with supercritical wild turmeric: two 500 mg capsules daily

Peripheral neuropathy

In this condition there is generalized sickness and damage to the peripheral nerves, that is the nerves that radiate out of the spinal column and end up innervating the extremities. The condition is manifested by stabbing pain and also burning and/or tingling. Peripheral neuropathy is exceedingly common in diabetics and is aggravated by uncontrolled blood sugar levels. In some cases the soreness and inflammation can be great and, thus, antiinflammatory drugs are prescribed, usually with modest if any effects.

Far more potent in curing this syndrome are antiiflammatory spice extracts, notably extracts of turmeric, wild rosemary, and wild oregano. As well, wild forms of turmeric are far more potent in reversing nerve-related inflammation than the commercial types. There is another major factor in this condition that is rarely addressed. This is B complex deficiency. In fact, peripheral neuropathy is one of the classical signs of the deficiency and represents a gross deficiency of niacin and thiamine, among others. Additionally, substances which deplete B vitamins must be avoided, notably caffeine, refined sugar, corn syrup, antibiotics, and anti-seizure medications.

Treatment protocol

- wild, raw turmeric extract with extracts of wild oregano and rosemary as sublingual drops: 20 or more drops twice daily

- whole food, raw turmeric extract with wild oregano, rosemary, and turmeric as 500 mg capsules: one or two capsules twice daily

- whole food B complex powder made from torula yeast, royal jelly, and rice bran: 2 or 3 T. daily

- organic turmeric powder complexed with cinnamon and ginger as turmeric milk, one or two cups daily (Note: the emulsified cinnamon aids in the control of blood sugar levels and, thus, reduces metabolic syndrome-related inflammation.

- Super-Strength organic cannabis extract with supercritical extract of wild oregano: rub topically and take internally, about 10 drops twice daily, a most powerful remedy for neuropathy

- Beta-caryophyllene-rich raw whole food cannabis extract with supercritical wild oregano: 10 or more drops twice daily

Reflex sympathetic dystrophy (RSD)

This is one of the most extreme of all nerve-related conditions known. It is a pain syndrome represented by a burning type of sensation, which may be severe, accompanied by tenderness and swelling. Usually occurring in the extremities it is associated with sensations of coolness, flushing, and discoloration, along with shiny-appearing skin. The syndrome is typically a consequence of trauma and involves damage to the sympathetic nerves. It may also be a side effect of surgery, stroke, and degenerative arthritis of the neck. It can also result from direct trauma to the extremities.

Because of its antinflammatory powers turmeric is an ideal therapeutic for this condition. It is, though, even more effective when combined with wild oregano oil therapy. As well, wild rosemary oil has great action against RSD.

Treatment protocol

- whole food turmeric sublingual drops with wild rosemary and ginger extracts: 20 or more drops three times daily; also use topically

- whole food, raw turmeric extract with wild oregano, rosemary, and turmeric as 500 mg capsules: one or two capsules twice daily

- wild oregano oil, Super-Strength formula: 20 drops twice daily, also rub topically several times daily

- bone-activating rubbing oil with wild rosemary, sage, and oregano oils: rub topically as needed

- Beta-caryophyllene-rich raw whole food cannabis extract with supercritical wild oregano: 10 or more drops twice daily

Brain and/or nerve injury

There is considerable data demonstrating the powers of turmeric in the healing of nerve damage, whether in the brain, spinal cord, or peripheral nerves. This relates to its antioxidant powers as well as its capacity to induce new cell growth. Regarding the latter it is the essential oil components, the turmerones, which exert the greatest capacity for regeneration.

Regeneration therapy is aided by the simultaneous intake of other key natural medicines, particularly cannabis extracts. Why is it so invaluable? This is largely because of its rich content of neurologically active compounds known as cannabinoids. The cannabinoids activate receptor sites in the brain and spinal cord, among other organ systems, leading to rather dramatic alterations in physiology. These actions lead to enhanced signaling between the neurons. Inflammatory reactions are modulated, and nerve cell repair, as well as regeneration, is induced.

One highly potent active ingredient of cannabis is the terpenoid, Beta-caryophyllene. This is, perhaps, the most powerful substance in cannabis and/or hemp, accounting for the notorious smell of marijuana. Beta-caryophyllene is also a primary active ingredient in wild oregano, hops, camomile, wild sage, cinnamon, and basil. It is a powerful dietary cannabinoid with significant actions as an antiinflammatory agent. As well, as demonstrated by a number of scientific studies the intake of this compound can induce the production of new neurons, a rare feat even for herbal medicines. Beta-caryophyllene is also found in turmeric, although cannabis, wild oregano, hops, basil, rosemary, and cinnamon are richer. Cannabis, though, is one of the most dense sources known. When combined with cannabidiol, that is CBD, Beta-caryophyllene exerts great powers within the brain, spinal cord, and brain stem to induce nerve cell repair. Of note, CBD oil is relatively low in Beta-caryophyllene. This is because the molecule is greatly destroyed or damaged by heat, and much heat, as well as solvent extraction, is applied in the making of this oil.

The most ideal types of cannabis extracts are those made through raw extraction, that is supercritical versions. Ideally, such extracts are made from organically raised industrial hemp, which is never solvent treated. This is a crucial issue. There is much solvent-treated CBD oil/hemp stalk extract on the market, much of it a residue of the textile industry, where refuse hemp is used as the basis.

This is why organically raised sources are so crucial. One such source is Hempanol, a certified organic extract of carefully and organically raised hemp, where the stalks are extracted with supercritial CO_2. The most therapeutic type contains also supercritical extract of wild oregano, as this, too, is a dense source of Beta-caryophyllene. As well, the wild oregano helps drive the cannabinoid molecules into the tissue, while also preventing their oxidation. Available in both regular and super-strength forms, it is also available as Hempanol CF, which, for the purist, is strictly organic, raw Beta-caryophyllene-rich cannabis extract, that is without the wild oregano.

Yet another therapeutic intervention is wild chaga, especially the raw forms. Raw chaga is available as water-soluble sublingual drops and capsules combined with wild birch bark and wild oregano. Both these forms are ideal for neuro-regeneration. Additionally, there are the aromatic waters of spices, notably the juice of wild oregano and the multiple spice/floral waters formula consisting of essences of wild oregano, sage, and rosemary, along with aromatic essences of rose petals and bitter orange blossoms. Taken regularly, these aromatic waters aid in the reversal of brain and nerve damage, including spinal cord injury and stroke-related damage.

Treatment protocol

- whole food turmeric sublingual drops with wild rosemary and ginger extracts: 20 or more drops three times daily; also use topically

- whole food, raw turmeric extract with wild oregano, rosemary, and turmeric as 500 mg capsules: one or two capsules twice daily

- Beta-caryophyllene-rich raw whole food cannabis extract with supercritical wild oregano: 20 or more drops twice daily

- Supercritical organic cannabis extract plus CO_2 extract of wild turmeric (that is Canacurmin) as mycellized sublingual drops: 20 or more drops twice daily

- aromatic waters complex with neroli orange, rose, wild rosemary, and wild oregano, that is Neuroloft: an ounce or more daily

Chapter Eight

The Major Killers

Can turmeric actually stall the progression of the major killers of Western society? More crucially, can it possibly reverse such disorders? Regarding heart disease, hypertension, diabetes, and cancer the fact is turmeric does offer significant benefits. Even so, it is most powerful when combined with other spices and whole food concentrates, which also have known, positive effects against such diseases, including cinnamon, ginger, wild oregano, wild rosemary, pomegranate, muscadine grape syrup/powder, and red grape concentrates. Additionally, wild chaga has positive actions against these syndromes, as do the plant enzymes bromelain and papain.

Heart disease

There are significant reports in the medical literature regarding the benefits of turmeric in the treatment of heart disease. This includes actions for improving the vital force of the heart and preventing, as well as reversing, arterial degeneration. There is also a significant capacity for blocking oxidative damage to the heart, which reduces the risks for coronary artery disease and myocardial infarction.

Excessive platelet activity increases the risks for heart disease, particularly coronary occlusion or stroke. In particular, compounds found in wild turmeric in the essential oil fraction block excessive platelet stickiness. This is through their action on arachidonic acid, which relates to collagen-induced platelet aggregation. To reverse this the intake of wild turmeric extract as mycellized sublingual drops is ideal.

Pomegranate offers additional protective benefits. So do red grape extracts or concentrates, for instance, red sour grape. Cinnamon protects heart function by reducing excessive fat and helping to regular blood sugar. Regular intake reduces the risks for syndrome X, which is associated with swings in blood sugar levels, high blood sugar counts, increase in abdominal, that is peritoneal, fat, and resistance to the actions of insulin.

There are also the roto-rooter-like complexes, bromelain and papain. These fruit-source enzymes, the bromelain deriving from pineapple, while the source for papain is papaya, help purge and cleanse the arterial walls from blockages. Through this, they improve the microcirculation throughout the body, including that through the coronary arteries. Turmeric is also associated with an improvement of microcirculation, all the way to the molecular level. Canabis extracts also aid heart function by causing a general state of relaxation, while also decreasing overall stress.

Treatment protocol

- whole food, Mediterranean-source pomegranate concentrate (that is PomaMax): 2 or more T. daily

- red sour grape powder: two or three capsules twice daily

- whole food, organic or wild turmeric powder: One tsp. or more daily

- whole food, raw, wild turmeric mycellized sublingual drops: 20 or more drops twice daily

- whole food resveratrol source, that is dried red sour grape: two or three capsules twice daily

- bromelain and papain complex with organic ginger and tumeric: two or three capsules twice daily on an empty stomach

- whole food vitamin complex with natural-source vitamin E and B complex, along with vitamins A and D (that is Purely-PAK), one packet daily

- Beta-caryophyllene-rich supercritical organic cannabis extract plus CO_2 extract of wild turmeric (that is Canacurmin) as mycellized sublingual drops: 10 or more drops twice daily

Hardening of the arteries

Turmeric and its extracts exert significant powers for protecting the arterial tree from chronic degeneration. These powerful natural medicines are also effective at reversing such disease, known as atherosclerosis. This condition is, essentially, a systematic breakdown of the arterial walls, represented by infiltration of these walls with cholesterol and calcium. Scarring or "sclerosis" also occurs. As a result, the arteries become stiff, and the loss of elasticity may lead to aneurysms and blood clots.

Stiff arteries are highly problematic. Normally, arteries are highly elastic. A lack of elasticity causes back-pressure, which leads to strain upon the heart. Put simply, this muscle must work considerably harder to pump blood against stiff, unyielding arteries. Plus, with elastic arteries there is another factor that is rarely considered: the role of germs. Smooth, rubbery arteries are not readily attacked by pathogens, while scarred ones with rough surfaces, and those infiltrated with pockets of cholesterol, are much more readily attacked. When there is inflammation in the arterial walls, they are also more readily infested.

Turmeric is a great aid, here. Its key compounds block the inflammatory processes that lead to arterial degeneration. Other natural complexes that block this degeneration include pomegranate, particularly its syrup-like concentrate, red sour grape powder, and oil of wild oregano. The wild oregano oil is invaluable, as it acts to purge pathogenic infestations. The fruit enzymes, bromelain and papain, offer powerful actions, largely as a result of their digestive actions. These enzymes act as nutritional "roto-rooter-like" agents, burrowing out blockages and corrosions.

Rosemary is another powerful spice medicine for blocking arterial degeneration. Rich in potent antioxidants, such as rosemarinic and carnosic acids, it helps halt oxidative destruction of the arteries, essentially preserving them from age-related hardening and stiffening.

A compelling new study demonstrates turmeric's immense powers versus arterial disorders. As demonstrated in the *Journal of Nutrition and Metabolism* one of the spice's active ingredients, curcumin, led to increased blood flow in human volunteers, similar to that seen with aspirin. Yet, the effect was modest, and this is because only the isolate form was used. The same positive results were seen from, incredibly, the ingestion of curry powder, which in a study published in *Nutrition Journal* also fully dilated the arteries.

Treatment protocol

- whole food, Mediterranean-source pomegranate concentrate (that is PomaMax): 2 or more T. daily

- whole food turmeric organic powder: tsp. daily

- whole food, raw, wild turmeric extract: one capsule twice daily

- whole food resveratrol source, that is dried red sour grape: two or three capsules twice daily

- bromelain and papain complex with organic ginger and tumeric: two or three capsules twice daily on an empty stomach

- oil of wild rosemary, edible type, daily use, in extra virgin olive oil: 20 drops twice daily

Diabetes

A severe pandemic this condition is largely a result of wrong diet. The greatest perpetrator is refined sugar, which causes systematic destruction of the digestive system, including the pancreas and liver, the two main organs involved in this disease. Other refined carbohydrates play a role, for instance, white flour and polished, white rice. All such 'foods' must be strictly avoided in order to control and/or reverse this disease. In contrast, the diet should be rich in healthy proteins, dark green leafy vegetables, and low-sugar fruit, like olives, avocadoes, tomatoes, limes, lemons, and strawberries as well as eggs and cheese. For more information about the ideal diet for reversing, as well as preventing, this condition see *Natural Cures for Diabetes*, same author.

While high carbohydrate intake is surely the main factor, there are still other elements that are responsible. These include psychic stress, exposure to toxins, and vaccinations. Infection may play a significant role in the onset of diabetes, especially in children and teenagers. That infection may result from a sudden-onset affliction, including immunizations. Some 50% of all cases of juvenile or Type 1 diabetes are caused by these noxious, destructive injections. The adult type is associated with inflammation, whether from infection or other causes. This may manifest as a kind of pre-diabetes, known as syndrome X. This syndrome is associated with much inflammation as well as a phenomenon known as "insulin resistance," the latter involving the deposition of peritoneal, or abdominal, fat. Here, reduction of the inflammation and weight loss help bring the condition under control.

There is a generalized benefit from the intake of turmeric for diabetes. This is because the spice helps combat insulin resistance. The positive effects are seen not merely with supplements but also with the whole food form, the raw spice, and also turmeric powder. It is also effective in reversing the symptoms of diabetic neuropathy.

Treatment protocol

- whole food turmeric extract with wild rosemary, wild oregano, and raw ginger extracts: 40 drops three times daily or two gelcaps two or three times daily

- whole food, organic turmeric powder: two tsp. twice daily

- raw, organic turmeric: at least one root daily

- wild, raw chaga extract as water soluble sublingual drops: 20 or more drops twice daily

- chaga-wild oregano-birch bark capsules: one or two twice daily

- juice or essence of wild oregano: one half ounce or more twice daily

- whole food vitamin complex with natural-source vitamin E, B complex, along with vitamins A and D (that is Purely-PAK), one packet daily

Cancer in general

Turmeric and its extracts are essential therapies in all forms of cancer. This is largely because of their antioxidant actions within the tissues. The spice's power is also related to its actions on the genes. Cancer is caused in part by a gross degeneration process of gene activity, where some 500 genes become corrupted. The signaling between these genes is in complete disarray. Turmeric helps regulate this by acting on the entire gene complex, unlike modern drugs, which target only single genes. While individual cancers are listed in the following section turmeric has a wide ranging power, sufficient to make it useful in all cancer types. Notes the highly conservative American Cancer Society:

> Laboratory studies have...shown that curcumin interferes with cancer development, growth, and spread (and that it) blocked the formation of cancer-causing enzymes in rodents.

The ACS also says it 'kills' cancer cells and reduces "tumor size." It's most powerful action appears to be against skin, colon, and breast cancer cells.

There are a number of other spices which are highly antitumor. These spices include ginger, black seed, and cumin, along with wild rosemary, oregano, and sage. Cannabis extract, too, possesses significant powers for cancer cell, as well as tumor, destruction. The ideal type of cannabis to consume for this purpose is complexed with extract of wild oregano, both from organic sources. The extract is superior to marijuana smoking, since it is rich in a special group of antitumor compounds, known as the terpenes. These are largely lost and destroyed from smoking. Yet, turmeric alone has great antitumor properties.

There is much published data specifically regarding turmeric and its preventive and curative role. Let us look, then, at this science to determine just how turmeric and its extracts function in cancer reversal and prevention.

Colorectal cancer

Perhaps the most ominous kind of cancer this is notoriously difficult to treat with orthodox methods. In fact, there is virtually no other treatment other than surgical resection, successful usually only in the early stages. Therefore, it must be treated and attacked in a different way: through botanical medicines. In a variety of clinical trials turmeric extracts, in particular, have shown efficacy. In human trials, consistently, there have been considerable benefits, measured by a reduction in cancer-associated metabolites such as M1G, a DNA adduct marker, along with a normalization of glutathione-S-transferase activity, the latter being a tumor-blocking enzyme system. The turmeric component curcumin was even found to be *concentrated into tumor tissue*, which helps block cancerous growth. Clearly, then, this turmeric pigment targets cancer cells.

In familial colon polyp syndrome, a precursor to colon cancer, turmeric extract, as curcumin was given, in this case, along with quercetin. The dosage was three times daily. Over a six-month period the number and size of the polyps decreased significantly.

Based on the overall results of these studies it has been determined, as made clear by A. Jacob and his group in *Mechanism of the Antiinflammatory Effect of Curcumin*, that curcumin is "efficacious for colorectal cancer..." The dose that is most effective is a minimum of 3.6 grams daily. The authoritative Cancer Research, UK, gives credence to curcumin therapy. Notes the organization, "A 2007 American study that combined curcumin with chemotherapy to treat bowel cancer cells in a laboratory showed that the combined treatment killed more cancer cells than chemotherapy alone."

The lower incidence of colon cancer in the Indian population confirms the findings of the studies. This is thought to be due to regular, even daily, use of turmeric powder in cooking. This would indicate that it is the regular use of this spice that is the key. Other cancers of the digestive organs where it has been shown to be effective include cancers of the esophagus and stomach. Through its antiinflammatory and antioxidant actions it also protects such organs from cancerous degeneration.

Wild oregano is a powerful adjunct for this condition. It acts to purge infectious agents, which are associated with the disease. For optimal results it must be used with the turmeric protocol. The birch tree medicine, wild chaga, has immense antitumor properties. It can be taken as a tea as well as capsules and sublingual drops. Regarding berries, in their raw form they are highly antitumor, particularly in colon cancer, where so little, medically, can be done. Organic berries are also effective but the wild are the most potent. The most potent of all berries for combating colon cancer is black raspberries, both as the whole berries and their raw extract. Freeze-dried powder is also active, while frozen berries are less potent.

Treatment protocol

- whole food turmeric extract with wild rosemary, wild oregano, and raw ginger extract: 40 drops three times daily or two gelcaps two or three times daily

- whole food, organic turmeric powder: two tsp. twice daily

- raw, organic turmeric: at least one root daily

- juice of wild oregano: a half ounce or more twice daily

- oil of wild oregano: five or more drops twice daily

- wild, raw chaga extract as sublingual drops: one or two droppersful twice daily

- wild, raw chaga capsules with wild oregano and birch bark: two capsules twice daily

- fresh juice of organic raspberries, blackberries, and/or strawberries: one half cup or more twice daily

- wild, raw eight berries complex: an ounce or more daily

- Rubinol wild, raw black raspberry drops: 40 or more drops twice daily

- Beta-caryophyllene-rich supercritical organic cannabis extract plus CO_2 extract of wild turmeric (that is Canacurmin) as mycellized sublingual drops: 20 or more drops twice daily

Pancreatic cancer

In this disease there is a great degree of oxidative damage suffered by the pancreas. This is why the intake of antioxidants helps ease the condition, along with all other disorders of this organ, including pancreatitis. Regarding the latter a study conducted in India found that oxidative damage within the pancreatic cells was definitely reduced by the combined intake of turmeric with black pepper extract. This was through the measurement of a significant reduction in levels of red blood cell MDA and also an increase in glutathione levels. In a trial conducted on 25 advanced pancreatic cancer patients there were positive consequences, with one patient having a marked shrinkage of the tumor mass. Yet, this was with the extracted type of curcumin. The results using wild turmeric and also the whole food complex are much more significant. In fact, the whole food type is associated with a significant reduction in Indian populations compared to Western societies.

Wild oregano is a most potent adjunct for pancreatic cancer. In particular, it helps purge infections associated with pancreatic disease, including infestations by molds, yeasts, and parasites. One parasite which plays a common role in damage to this organ is intestinal or liver flukes. These flukes may attack the head of the pancreas causing inflammation, ultimately provoking cancer. It is the juice of oregano which is most effective agains this and may outright reverse the condition. For optimal results it should be combined with edible, daily use oil of wild oregano. Berries are also highly effective versus this condition and are often tolerated when no other food can be consumed. In their raw state berries contain biologically active enzymes, which assist digestion, taking the strain off the pancreas. Enzymes, in particular, are valuable versus this condition, both in treatment and prevention.

Treatment protocol

- whole food turmeric extract with wild rosemary, wild oregano, and raw ginger extract: 40 drops three times daily or two gelcaps two or three times daily

- whole food, organic turmeric powder: two tsp. twice daily

- raw, organic turmeric: at least one root daily

- juice/essence of wild oregano: a half ounce or more twice daily

- oil of wild oregano, edible type, as drops under the tongue: five to ten drops two or three times daily

- enzyme plus spice complex including protease plus bromelain and papain: two or three capsules with meals; in severe cases up to five capsules may be taken with meals

- fresh juice of organic raspberries, blackberries, and/or strawberries: one half cup or more twice daily

- Rubinol wild, raw black raspberry drops: 40 or more drops twice daily

- Raspenol red and black raspberry powder: heaping teaspoonful twice daily

Lung cancer

This pandemic is due to a number of factors, one of which is, certainly, tobacco smoking, while another is exposure to second hand smoke. Asbestos contamination is a cause, and so is infection of the lungs by vaccine viruses, notably SV40. Air pollution plays a significant role. There is a factor which is rarely considered, which is chronic infection of the lungs. The infectious agents include mold, yeast, and parasites. Regarding parasites, the most destructive and dangerous element is lung flukes. Untreated, these flukes cause such an immense degree of inflammation that cancer readily develops. Flukes in the lungs may have their origins in the gut or liver, from which they are seeded.

Tobacco smoking, particularly the smoking of cigarettes, is the primary cause of this disease. Cigarette smoke, for instance, incites great oxidation within the body, depleting its antioxidant reserves. In particular, it causes a massive depletion of vitamin C, as each cigarette destroy as much as 40 mg of the vitamin, which is about the daily minimum intake. Tobacco smoke also depletes vitamin E, along with the antioxidant enzyme glutatione. What an exceedingly destructive habit this is, harming not only the smoker but also all those closely associated. Nicotene is one of the most deadly natural chemicals known. No one should purposely exposure their bodies to it. Smokers must quit precipitously and categorically to avoid senseless harm to themselves and also any who are in close proximity. Second-hand smoke is a proven cause of lung cancer; how truly criminal it is to smoke, while knowingly causing harm to others.

Even so, turmeric is an ideal neutraceutical complex for purging smoking related toxins, including nicotine. To achieve this it is best to take it on a daily basis, both supplementally and as a whole foods. One of the most ideal purging agents in this regard is the mycellized sublingual drops.

It should always be kept in mind that it does not take much to induce programmed cell death in cancerous tissue. It is merely necessary to consume the correct therapy for inducing this, and the spices, as well as cannabis extract, are the most potent in this regard. In this regard the combined supplement, Canacurmin, is an ideal therapeutic choice.

Treatment protocol

- whole food turmeric extract with wild rosemary, wild oregano, and raw ginger extract: 20 to 40 drops three times daily or two gelcaps two or three times daily

- whole food, organic turmeric powder: two tsp. twice daily

- raw, organic turmeric: at least one root daily

- juice/essence of wild oregano: an ounce or more twice daily

- oil of wild oregano, edible type, as drops under the tongue: five to ten drops three or more times daily

- multiple spice complex capsules consisting of dried oils of wild oregano and sage plus dried cinnamon and cumin oils: two or more capsules two or three times daily

- whole food vitamin C complex with wild camu camu and acerola cherry: a minimum of two capsules twice daily

- a combination of lemon and orange juice (or grapefruit juice): four ounces twice daily (as a vitamin C source especially valuable for smokers)

- whole food vitamin E complex from sunflowerseed oil fortified with Austrian-source Styrian pumpkinseed oil: one or more capsules twice daily

- Supercritical cannabis extract with raw supercritical turmeric extract plus curcuminoid resin (that is Canacurmin): 20 or more drops twice daily

Lymphoma

In this condition the untenable has occurred. In most cases the body has become infected by foreign viruses, not from other humans but, rather, from monkeys. The source of the infestation is Rhesus monkey macaques, brought to this country by criminal elements in the pharmaceutical industry. The purpose for these animals was to infect them with strains of polio viruses, since these viruses require animal matter in which to grow. This was in order to create the polio vaccination scam. Tissues from the infected monkeys were harvested, including their testes and kidneys from which a solution was made that was then put into the vaccine.

Yet, here is the dilemma; that vaccine solution was infected not only with live polio viruses but also with various monkey pathogens, including simian virus 40, known as SV40. In fact, SV40 is a direct cause of lymphoma, responsible for up to 60% of all cases. This has been demonstrated by a wide range of investigators, including Loyola's Michelle Carbone and researchers at MD Anderson. The source of the infection is various vaccines, the polio sugar cube being most notorious. The majority of victims are those who received the 1950s-through 1970s-era polio sugar cubes, as well as shots, which were extensively contaminated.

In order to cure this disease the foreign virus and/or viruses must be thoroughly purged. Turmeric helps in this regard; however, it is necessary to consume spices which are more potent in antiseptic capacity. The most potent of all is oil of wild oregano. The ideal type to use is the daily use form emulsified in extra virgin olive oil.

In fact, this oil in the Super-Strength form has been used successfully to purge this virus from the body and, thus, take lymphoma into remission. The more aggressive the wild oregano is used, the better is the potential for a complete and rapid cure. SV40 is no contest for this wild spice extract, especially if combined with wild turmeric concentrate and also the heavy consumption of the organic spice. Cumin and cinnamon are also optimal purging agents for this virus, found in the multiple spice capsules and sublingual oil.

Treatment protocol

- juice/essence of wild oregano: an ounce or more twice daily

- oil of wild oregano, edible type, as drops under the tongue: 20 to 40 drops or more three or more times daily; also rub topically on any swollen lymph nodes as well as on the bottoms of the feet, shins, top of the thighs, and up-and-down the spine; keep in mind when using the edible type (P73) there is no limit to the amount that can be taken

- multiple spice complex capsules consisting of dried oils of wild oregano and sage plus dried cinnamon and cumin oils: three capsules three or more times daily

- wild, raw turmeric extract as 500 mg capsules: three or more capsules twice daily

- whole food turmeric extract with wild rosemary, wild oregano, and raw ginger extract: 40 drops three times daily or two gelcaps two or three times daily

- whole food vitamin complex with natural-source vitamin E, B complex, along with vitamins A and D (that is Purely-PAK), one packet daily

- Beta-caryophyllene-rich supercritical, organic cannabis extract plus CO_2 extract of wild oregano (that is Hempanol): 20 or more drops twice daily

Leukemia

While it seems unfathomable leukemia is largely a man-made disease. The primary cause is none other than that vile, noxious medical intervention, vaccinations. According to one prominent medical journal, *Cancer Research*, some 90% of all cases are vaccine-induced. The same was determined by Robert Mendolson, who found that in his pediatric practice it was inoculations which caused the potentially fatal disease. He noted that the incidence for disease sky-rocketed in direct association with the introduction of mass vaccination.

The inoculations lead to infection of the cells by a host of pathogenic viruses. These viruses ultimately attack the nuclear material of the cell, the actual DNA strands, causing the induction of this disease.

Even so, the role of nutritional deficiency must not be neglected, as there are typically deficits of a wide range of nutrients in this condition, notably vitamin C, vitamin A, and the B complex. As well, infection of the body by parasites is a common precursor for leukemia, with infestation by intestinal and liver flukes predominating.

In many cases the victims suffer from a weakness in the hormonal system known as adrenal insufficiency. When the adrenal glands are incapacitated—when they are unable to produce sufficient amounts of their secretions, known as corticosteroids—the body is more vulnerable to infection by the leukemia-causing pathogens.

Turmeric is one of many natural complexes that can prove lifesaving for leukemia. Other crucial spices include wild rosemary, sage, oregano, along with cumin, cinnamon, and clove buds.

Taking into account children and teenagers as major victims of this disease the protocol emphasizes liquids and powders. When capsules are mentioned, their contents can be emptied and placed into food or smoothies. As well, the total body purging agent is listed as a means to eradicate intestinal flukes.

Treatment protocol

- whole food turmeric extract with wild rosemary, wild oregano, and raw ginger extract: 40 drops three times daily or two gelcaps two or three times daily

- whole food, organic turmeric powder: two tsp. twice daily

- raw, organic turmeric: at least one root daily

- juice/essence of wild oregano: an ounce or more twice daily

- oil of wild oregano, edible type, as drops under the tongue: five to ten drops three or more times daily

- multiple spice complex capsules consisting of dried oils of wild oregano and sage plus dried cinnamon and cumin oils: two or more capsules twice daily

- whole food, wild-source vitamin C complex with wild camu camu and acerola cherry: tsp. of the powder twice daily or two or three capsules twice daily

- whole food fatty salmon oil rich in vitamins A and D: tsp. twice daily

- total body purging agent with black seed oil and wild greens extracts: T. twice daily and for adults, an ounce or more daily (with meals or, preferably, on an empty stomach)

- digestive enzyme complex with bromelain and papain plus spice concentrates: one or two with each meal

- Beta-caryophyllene-rich supercritical, organic cannabis extract plus CO_2 extract of wild oregano (that is Hempanol): 20 or more drops twice daily

Multiple myeloma

There is considerable evidence that this disease is readily treatable with turmeric therapy. This may be related to its actions to directly modulate the genes, leading to programmed cell death of cancer cells. A 2014 French study indicates this, where it was discovered that the pigment curcumin was active in causing myeloma cell death. This is supported by the work of MD Anderson, where a patient case is recorded of a woman put into remission on its turmeric treatment protocol. Regardless, curcumin, as well as the whole food turmeric complex, synergize any drug treatment for this condition and, thus, are a must in any anti-myeloma plan.

Treatment protocol

- whole food turmeric extract with wild rosemary, wild oregano, and raw ginger extract: 40 drops three times daily or two gelcaps two or three times daily

- whole food, organic turmeric powder: two tsp. twice daily

- raw, organic turmeric: at least one root daily

- juice/essence of wild oregano: an ounce or more twice daily

- oil of wild oregano, edible type, as drops under the tongue: ten or more drops three or more times daily

- whole food, raw cannabis extract with wild supercritical oregano: three capsules twice daily

- Beta-caryophyllene-rich supercritical organic cannabis extract plus CO_2 extract of wild turmeric (that is Canacurmin) as mycellized sublingual drops: 10 or more drops twice daily

Breast cancer

This condition is far easier to treat that most people realize. This is particularly true if it is caught early before chemotherapy, surgery, or radiotherapy is applied. Regardless, by no means should the breasts ever become cancerous. This means that, in fact, it is a preventable disease.

Diet plays a major role in its cause, as does emotional factors. Abusive relationships do bring it on, particularly a lack of a truly loving interaction. The emotional distress from an unloyal spouse who is having extra-marital affairs may be so significant that the condition results. This is particularly true of those who internalize it, that is who hold their anger and frustration deeply within and who do not voice or vent their rage: or despair. It happens more commonly with the person who essentially says to the self, "What was wrong with me? Wasn't I good enough? How could he do this to me?"

Yet another factor is trauma. A direct strike to the breast can cause such a degree of corruption that a tumor may develop. Alcohol consumption is directly associated, even wine. In fact, the regular consumption of this beverage by vulnerable women, even as little as two glasses per week, increases the cancer risks by as much as five-fold. Alcohol is a fat-loving solvent. Thus, it directly attacks the mostly fatty breast tissue. Here are the risks for breast cancer induction through wine consumption:

• two glasses per week: 3x increased risk
• three to five glasses per week: 4x increased risk
• about a glass per day: 5x increased risk
• two glasses per day: 5 to 6-fold increased risk

Alcohol also depletes the B complex, vitamin C, and vitamin E, all of which are required for healthy breast tissue as well as for the metabolism of sex hormones. There is also the issue of the so-called estrogen dominant woman. No doubt, these women are more vulnerable to breast cancer induction. Yet, alcohol aggravates this by disrupting the liver's ability to detoxify this hormone. What's more, nutritional deficiency plays a role, as vitamin A, vitamin C, vitamin E, and the B complex are necessary for proper estrogen production as well as metabolism.

The thyroid gland is directly tied to this disease process, that is the existence of hypothyroidism or impaired thyroid function. Healthy function of this gland helps keep the breasts supple, preventing congestion. With hypothyroidism there is a thick matter which may develop within the breasts, along with an increased risk for cysts. The resulting congestion and inflammation can act as a precursor to the disease. It is the iodine-based thyroid secretions, diiodotyrosine and thyroxine, which keep the breasts in a normal, semi-fluid state. This is why iodine therapy and/or the consumption of kelp acts as a breast cancer preventive as does the regular intake of a thyroid-supporting supplement complex.

In addition to turmeric wild rosemary and oregano are highly powerful for reversing breast cancer. So is wild sage. This is true of the herbs and also the properly sourced wild spice oils. Other spices with anti-breast cancer powers include fennel and anise. These two spices directly block the toxicity of noxious forms of estrogen.

Royal jelly is yet another key anti-breast cancer complex. Its steroids create balanced estrogen production and detoxification. Plus, royal jelly makes the breasts firmer and more supple, while preventing their degeneration. The most powerful type of supplemental royal jelly is the 3x type. Typically, royal jelly powder comes in a 1x form, as it is diluted due to cost factors. An ideal formula would contain wild sage and rosemary, which stabilize royal jelly and make it more effective as an adrenal tonic and also for enhancing breast health.

Treatment protocol

- whole food, raw, wild turmeric extract with wild rosemary and oregano: two or more capsules twice daily

- raw, organic turmeric: at least one root daily

- juice/essence of wild oregano: an ounce or more twice daily

- oil of wild oregano, edible type, as drops under the tongue: five to ten drops twice daily; also apply topically as often as possible, avoiding the sensitive nipple

- 3x royal jelly capsules with wild rosemary and sage: two or more capsules twice daily

- whole food vitamin complex with natural-source vitamin E, B complex, along with vitamins A and D (that is Purely-PAK), one or, preferably, two packets daily

- raw, wild graviola leaf extract: tsp. daily or every other day depending on tolerance

- raw, organic sacha inchi oil: 2 T. daily

- Beta-caryophyllene-rich supercritical organic cannabis extract plus CO_2 extract of wild turmeric (that is Canacurmin) as mycellized sublingual drops: 10 or more drops twice daily

Prostate cancer

In prostate cancer there is both a role of noxious, toxic hormones and also invasive infections. Because it is so deeply set within the body it is vulnerable to infectious attack. This may play a greater role in the cause and progression of this disease than mere hormones alone.

With aging there is a decline in testosterone production. This leads to a weakening of the prostate tissue, making it vulnerable to both degeneration and infectious onslaught. Turmeric can help block this by boosting sex hormone production while also squelching oxidative damage to the organ. As this spice is only a modest antiseptic it is necessary to consume powerful germ-killing spice extracts, for instance, the edible oils of wild oregano and sage as well as cumin and bay leaf. In most instances the oil of wild oregano alone suffices to purge any hidden or overt prostatic infections.

There is yet another natural medicine that is essential for the treatment of this condition: crude unprocessed pumkinseed oil. Of all types of such oil the most potent and effective for this condition is the Styrian type, which is a production of Austria. Known as Pumpkinol, it is a reliable treatment for swollen, inflamed, and even cancerous prostate conditions. Styrian pumkinseed oil contains sterols that inactivate the notorious prostate cancer-inducing hormone, dihydrotestosterone or DHT. This natural medicine is available as the whole food oil and also in capsule form as a concentrate combined with wild oregano, wild rosemary, and St. John's wort. Pumpkinol itself is a novel supplement, as it is fortified with oil of fennel. This spice oil also blocks the toxic effects of DHT. The combination of wild, raw turmeric extract, oil of wild oregano, and crude unprocessed pumpkinseed oil complexed with oil of fennel is a most powerful therapeutic approach to reverse all prostatic conditions.

For prostate disorders and also for prevention focusing on only a high-powered, extract-based supplement is not the answer. Only the whole food forms can be relied upon to achieve a thorough cure. For instance, turmeric powder, when combined with cruciferous vegetables, has been shown to, slow down or even halting the growth of existing tumor cells.

Treatment protocol

- juice/essence of wild oregano: an ounce or more twice daily

- oil of wild oregano, edible type, as drops under the tongue: five to ten drops twice daily

- raw, unprocessed Styrian pumpkinseed oil fortified with fennel oil: one T. daily for mild-to-moderate cases and for severe cases, 2 to 4 T. daily

- Styrian pumpkinseed oil concenrate, 10:1, as capsules with saw palmetto berry and wild oregano: two capsules twice daily

- whole food turmeric extract with wild rosemary, wild oregano, and raw ginger extract: 40 drops three times daily or two gelcaps two or three times daily

- whole food, raw, wild turmeric extract with wild rosemary and oregano: one or more capsules twice daily

- Beta-caryophyllene-rich supercritical, organic cannabis extract plus CO_2 extract of wild oregano (that is Hempanol): 20 or more drops twice daily

Skin cancer

In all skin cancers turmeric plays a considerable role. Other powerful natural medicines include wild oregano and rosemary, particularly their emulsified spice oils. Yet another effective treatment is wild, raw berries extract. The berries extract is curative taken internally but also applied topically. Wild berries contain naturally occurring cyanide compounds, which are destructive to skin cancer cells. Turmeric, too, is highly destructive. The mycellized drops can be used as a topical therapy as well as taken sublingually. They offer the benefit of containing oils of wild oregano and rosemary, which are also highly effective anticancer agents.

Treatment protocol

- whole food, raw, wild turmeric extract with wild rosemary and oregano: two capsules twice daily or take internally, 20 or more drops twice daily

- wild, raw chaga cream in a beeswax base with aromatic spice oils: apply topically as needed; the turmeric can be applied for half the day, followed by the chaga at night

- wild, raw multiple berries extract as a 2-ounce dropper bottle: take 40 drops twice daily under the tongue

Melanoma

Turmeric has a unique property versus melanoma. It helps reverse the excessive activity of the melanocytes. Another natural medicine which does so is wild chaga. As well, wild birch bark has this power of modulating melanocyte activity. Wild oregano is an effective anti-melanoma agent. The Super-Strength form is a highly aggressive formula for destroying these lesions. It will potentiate any anticancer turmeric therapy.

It is curious to note that this disease is also known as fungoid. Then, is there a parasitic role by various invasive molds and yeasts? It is a certainty that the excessive intake of refined sugar increases the risks for invasive melanoma and that curtailing it stalls its growth. This is why wild oregano oil is so effective in the treatment of this condition. It purges the associated fungus, causing self-destruction of the cancerous cells.

Treatment protocol

- whole food, raw, wild turmeric extract with wild rosemary and oregano: two capsules twice daily

- wild juice/essence of wild oregano: an ounce twice daily

- Super-Strength oil of wild oregano: take 10 or more drops twice daily and also apply topically by saturating Telfa (gauze) padsor cotton and applying; may be applied with mycellized turmeric drops

- whole food vitamin complex with natural-source vitamin E, B complex, along with vitamins A and D (that is Purely-PAK), one or, preferably, two packets daily

- wild, raw chaga sublingual drops: 40 to 60 drops twice daily, also consume wild chaga tea, ideally with pulverized birch and tamarack bark

- wild tamarack, that is larch, bark tea (LovelyLarch Tea): two or more cups daily

- Beta-caryophyllene-rich supercritical organic cannabis extract plus CO_2 extract of wild turmeric (that is Canacurmin) as mycellized sublingual drops: 10 or more drops twice daily

Chapter Nine

Digestive Disorders

Digestive disorders are another major arena for turmeric's medicinal powers. In fact, this is largely where it exerts its most novel, as well as dependable, capacities. There is great benefit to the entire digestive process through turmeric intake, and this occurs with all its forms, the raw, organic root, the root juice, the whole, powder spice, and the whole food concentrates and/or extracts.

Gastric and/or duodenal disorders

In this category there are the conditions gastritis, esophageal reflux, also known as gastroesophageal reflux or GERD, gastric ulcer, duodenal inflammation, and duodenal ulcer. Clearly, all such syndromes are associated with inflammation. Therefore, whole food turmeric and its extracts prove to be effective modalities. Versus the chemical isolates it is these forms alone which should be used for disorders of the digestive tract. For instance, in one study it was found that turmeric powder caused an increase in the production of intestinal wall-protecting mucous, whereas *purified curcumin failed to achieve this.*

Any irritation of the digestive system responds to turmeric therapy. Both the spice and its whole food, chemical-free extracts have an action known as carminative. This means that there is the elimination of gas, bloating, and distention. An ideal therapeutic method is to add a teaspoonful of turmeric to a cup of whole fat, high-quality, probiotic-rich yogurt and consume this once or twice daily. It may also be added to liquid kefir, consuming a cup twice per day, each cup containing a teaspoon of the powder. Whole food supplements are also effective for this, especially those containing ginger. Regarding turmeric supplements with black pepper isolates for digestive disorders this may not be ideal, since such powerful extracts readily cause gastric irritation.

In addition, for the full range of digestive conditions wild oregano is an invaluable treatment. Most cases of stomach and/or esophageal disorders are caused by bacterial infection, notably by the notorious pathogen H. pylori. Both the oil and essence of wild oregano obliterate this germ, causing a remission and/or elimination of the symptoms.

Treatment protocol

- whole food turmeric extract with wild rosemary, wild oregano, and raw ginger extract: 20 or more drops three times daily or two gelcaps twice daily

- whole food, wild & organic turmeric powder: two tsp. twice daily

- raw, organic turmeric: at least one root daily

- juice or essence of wild oregano: T. twice daily

- oil of wild oregano, edible type, daily use: five drops twice daily

- digestive enzyme complex with ginger and cardomom, along with proteolytic enzymes (that is Gastronex): two or three capsules with each meal

Gallbladder disease

Turmeric is one of many natural complexes which are effective against gallbladder disease. Studies have shown that it has a generally positive action, increasing the synthesis of bile while also stimulating gallbladder contractions. It is not alone in these powers. In fact, its actions are potentiated through the intake of herbal bitters, including bitter greens. Among the bitter greens the most effective gallbladder purging complexes are wild dandelion and burdock. Both these plants contain substances, for instance, waxes and saponins, which activate the synthesis of bile, while also inducing gallbladder contraction.

Regarding gallstones, it is best to not take turmeric alone. In fact, it must ideally be taken with extracts of bitter greens. Yet another potent bitter is wild dandelion root. Black seed oil is also invaluable in this regard, acting both as a bile- and gallstone-purge. The total body purging agent is a mixture of such bitter greens plus dandelion root with black seed oil plus oils of rosemary and fennel. It is a potent, effective purging solution for gallstone overload. In some cases through the intake of this solution dozens, even hundreds, of stones are dumped. The wild greens, as well as dandelion root, in this supplement are raw, and that is why it is so effective. Only North American Herb & Spice, world leader in high quality natural supplements, makes such wild, raw products.

For gallbladder attacks fennel has special properties. It calms spasticity, with the edible oil of this spice being particularly potent. It may be taken as sublingual drops directly during the attack to halt it.

Another aromatic bitter is essence of neroli orange. The essence is made from the blossoms of this type of orange tree, which grows along the Mediterranean ocean. Long used for calming the nerves it also helps calm or balance gallbladder contractions, while stimulating the flow of bile. Orange blossom essence is available in a 12-ounce bottle as Essence of Orange Blossom and is an ideal addition to liver-gallbladder cleansing protocols.

Treatment protocol

- whole food total body purging agent with black seed oil, wild, raw nettles extract, wild burdock/dandelion extracts: an ounce or more in the a.m. on an empty stomach

- whole food, raw, wild dandelion plus root extract: one half ounce twice daily

- whole food, organic turmeric powder: two tsp. twice daily

- raw, organic turmeric: at least one root daily

- edible oil of fennel: five to ten drops under the tongue as needed

- whole food, raw, wild turmeric extract with wild rosemary and oregano: two capsules twice daily

- Essence of Orange Blossoms: an ounce once or twice daily, ideally taken with the total body purging agent

Rectal inflammation (proctitis)

It has been long known that turmeric is effective against this condition. The turmeric pigments and resins coat the entire digestive tract, greatly reducing irritation and inflammation. These pigments are particularly valuable for the lower colon and rectum, which they do reach intact. This may explain the effectiveness of whole food turmeric extracts and the whole spice for hemorrhoids. In fact, for any kind of irritation in the rectum or anus turmeric is the cure. Other spices which reduce rectal irritation include fennel, ginger, and wild oregano.

Treatment protocol

- whole food turmeric extract with wild rosemary, wild oregano, and raw ginger extract: 40 drops three times daily or two gelcaps two or three times daily

- whole food, organic turmeric powder: two tsp. twice daily

- raw, organic turmeric: at least one root daily

- edible oil of fennel: five to ten drops under the tongue as needed

- oil of wild oregano: three to five drops under the tongue twice daily

- Beta-caryophyllene-rich supercritical, organic cannabis extract plus CO_2 extract of wild oregano (that is Hempanol): 20 or more drops twice daily

Crohn's disease/ulcerative colitis

As an antiinflammatory agent turmeric and its extracts are an essential therapy for Crohn's disease. This is because they can effectively replace toxic drugs used for the condition, including methotrexate and Prednisone. For optimal results the infection related to this disease must also be dealt with. It is now confirmed that Crohn's disease is directly caused by chronic infection, usually from various fungi, including species of candida and also tuberculosis. A slow-growing type of TB has been cultured from the intestinal walls of Crohn's victims. The likely source is tainted vaccinations given during childhood. In this case turmeric therapy alone is not sufficient to resolve it. The infections must be simultaneously purged. This is through the intake of oil of wild oregano as well as its aromatic essence.

Even so, in all its forms turmeric is invaluable, as it systematically attacks the colitis-related inflammatory processes. In a 2006 study, which was double-blinded and placebo-controlled, curcumin helped induce remission in ulcerative colitis patients. A 2013 paper concluded it is a highly "promising new therapeutic option for the treatment of gastrointestinal and hepatic diseases..."

Treatment protocol

- whole food turmeric extract with wild rosemary, wild oregano, and raw ginger extract: 40 drops three times daily or two gelcaps two or three times daily

- whole food, organic turmeric powder: two tsp. twice daily

- raw, organic turmeric: at least one root daily

- whole, crude, crushed wild oregano with Rhus coriaria (that is OregaMax capsules): two twice daily

- juice of wild oregano (P73): one or, ideally, two ounces twice daily

- oil of wild oregano, SuperStrength formula: 5 drops under the tongue multiple times daily

- plant-source probiotic formula, that is Ecologic 500: half tsp. or more at night in a glass of luke-warm water

- cold-pressed oil of black seed with fennel seed oil: one ounce daily

- Beta-caryophyllene-rich supercritical organic cannabis extract plus CO_2 extract of wild turmeric (that is Canacurmin) as mycellized sublingual drops: 10 or more drops twice daily

Colon polyps

Wild, raw turmeric and/or its extracts has a great power on the prevention of colonic diseases, including pre-cancerous and cancerous changes. As well, whole food turmeric powder also exerts this action, especially if emulsified, for instance, as turmeric milk. In fact, all the spices have actions against polyps, both as curative agents and also for prevention. Golden or turmeric milk combines three or more of these, notably turmeric, ginger, and cinnamon, in some cases black pepper and/or cardamom.

Probiotics also aid in the reversal of these lesions. Curiously, many spices actually boost the levels of such good, healthy bacteria. However, their concentrates, that is spice oils, may reduce the levels: at least temporarily. Other complexes that boost probiotic levels include raw yacon and tamarack or larch bark. The latter is available in ChagaBlack tea and also Lovely-Larch tea. Both wild chaga and larch bark aid in the eradication of colon polyps.

To obliterate the polyps rather large doses are needed, at least initially. It takes about 90 days to purge them, although in some cases where there is a great multiplicity of them it may take longer.

Treatment protocol

- whole food turmeric extract with wild rosemary, wild oregano, and raw ginger extract: 20 to 40 drops three times daily or two gelcaps two or three times daily

- juice of wild oregano (P73): ounce once or, preferably, twice daily

- oil of wild oregano, SuperStrength, daily use formula: 10 or more drops twice daily

- plant-source probiotic formula, that is Ecologic 500: half tsp. or more at night in a glass of luke-warm water

- raw yacon syrup: a tsp. daily

- ChagaBlack tea: two or more cups daily

- turmeric milk within added coconut fat: drink one cup twice daily

- Beta-caryophyllene-rich supercritical organic cannabis extract plus CO_2 extract of wild turmeric (that is Canacurmin) as mycellized sublingual drops: 10 or more drops twice daily

Chronic constipation

There can be nothing worse for the body than chronic inability to eliminate wastes. This is particularly true of intestinal waste. Impaired elimination of this highly toxic matter destabilizes the body, increasing the risks for a wide range of diseases and syndromes, including chronic allergy, inflammatory skin disorders, lung disease, hemorrhoids, varicose veins, liver disorders, colitis/irritable bowel syndrome, stomach conditions, and cancer. Turmeric is one of the most invaluable natural medicines as an overall detoxification agent. It helps purge the body of toxins in all arenas, including via the colon. It is an invaluable decongesting agent for not only the colon but also the gallbladder and liver. It is even more potent in this regard when combined with ginger and cinnamon.

Turmeric decongests the intestines, improving both digestion and elimination. Both ginger and turmeric stimulate digestive juices, aiding in the processing and assimilation of food. There are other natural cures that are needed for decongesting the bowel. These natural remedies include wild, raw dandelion root/leaf extract, wild, raw berry extract, and black seed oil. For optimal relief of chronic constipation these remedies should be included in the protocol.

Treatment protocol

- whole food, organic turmeric powder: two tsp. twice daily
- raw, organic turmeric: at least one root daily

- turmeric milk: one or more cups daily; for extreme cases consume three or more cups daily

- wild, raw turmeric extract with ginger and wild rosemary: one capsule twice daily

- raw, wild dandelion root plus leaf extract: one or more ounces daily

- oil of Mediterranean black seed: one ounce daily

- wild, raw multiple berries complex, that is Super-5-Berries: one or more ounces daily

- beets, either raw or cooked: consume as many as possible

Pancreatitis

This condition is one of the most painful and, in fact, dangerous of all digestive disorders. Causes include toxic insults, for instance, excessive alcohol consumption and also severe stress. Yet another factor is infection, with intestinal parasites being the primary agents.

While it is a medical emergency, still, spice therapy is indicated. This is the most effective way to ease the symptoms. The wild oregano oil helps purge infectious agents, which aids in achieving a remission. In particular, the juice of wild oregano is ideal and is usually well tolerated. People with extra sensitive systems may wish to start with the juice, sipping on it a little at a time and then add the oil later. The key is to stabilize the inflammation with powerful antioxidants, and spices, including turmeric, effectively do so. Turmeric is exceedingly well tolerated in acute cases and should be taken in all its forms. It is completely safe to give even in the midst of severe, acute cases. In fact, it may prove lifesaving by fully and rapidly halting the pancreatitis-associated inflammatory reaction.

It is also necessary to apply enzyme therapy. The pancreas is the body's enzyme factor. In pancreatitis there is insufficiency of production. Through the intake of enzymes the pancreas is rested and, thus, a full recovery in its function is more readily achieved.

Treatment protocol

- whole food turmeric extract with wild rosemary, wild oregano, and raw ginger extract: 40 drops three times daily or two gelcaps two or three times daily

- whole food, organic turmeric powder: two tsp. twice daily

- raw, organic turmeric: at least one root daily

- whole food digestive enzyme complex combined with spice concentrates, that is Gastronex: two or three capsules with each meal

- juice of wild oregano, a most important natural cure for this condition: start slowly, and sip on it, then, after a day or two take an ounce once or twice daily

- raw, wild dandelion root plus leaf extract: one or more ounces daily

Hemorrhoids

A plague of modern humanity this is largely a consequence of stool habits, where the individual is unable to fully evacuate bowel contents. It is also related to an overall lack of fiber intake, resulting in hardened stools and/or straining at the stool as a result of impaction. Fiber helps force a more natural evacuation by increasing the girth of the stool. It also acts as a prebiotic for stimulating the growth of stool-bulking healthy bacteria. Moreover, fiber helps hold water within the colon, preventing dehydration of bowel contents.

Another issue is the Western toilet, which is too high for achievement of healthy, normal evacuation.

There may be associated nutritional deficiencies, for instance, a lack of vitamin C and bioflavonoids. Vitamin K deficit is also involved, as is a lack of magnesium. There may also be a deficit in the levels of probiotics, which decreases the bulk of the stool.

Turmeric is a boon for this condition. All of its forms are effective treatments. It can also be used topically as a hemorrhoidal paste. As a traditional Ayurvedic remedy this paste consists of mustard oil or, preferably, oil of black seed combined with turmeric powder and onion juice. Other antihemorrhoidal therapies include primitive-made raspberry root plus leaf syrup, known as RaspaSyrup, and freeze-dried raspberry powder. Known as RaspaMax because of its dense source of tissue-toning tannins it is an ideal adjunct to the wild raspberry syrup. Also, take 3 tablespoonsful of turmeric powder daily, while also taking the extract as sublingual drops and/or gelcaps. The topical treatment is so powerful that, usually, all bleeding is halted: within an hour or two.

Additionally, it is necessary in reversing this to increase fiber intake. There are number of fiber supplements on the market, which can increase the bulk of the stool. This causes an easing in elimination, while reducing straining, which can have a major impact on eliminating this disorder.

Note: the hand-made, specialized anti-hemorrhoidal complex called RaspaSyrup, made from boiled down wild raspberry leaves and roots, is only available online: www.cassingram.com.

Treatment protocol

- whole food turmeric extract with wild rosemary, wild oregano, and raw ginger extract: 40 drops three times daily or two gelcaps two or three times daily

- whole food, organic turmeric powder: two tsp. twice daily

- raw, organic turmeric: at least one root daily

- turmeric milk, ideally with ginger and cinnamon: one or more cups daily; for extreme cases consume three or more cups daily

- topical turmeric paste: make an appropriate paste of turmeric, coconut fat, and water and apply, as needed; it can be inserted into the rectum as well

- plant-source probiotic formula, that is Ecologic 500: half tsp. or more at night in a glass of luke-warm water

- whole food digestive enzyme complex combined with spice concentrates, that is Gastronex: two or three capsules with each meal

- hand-made syrup of wild raspberry root and leaves: T. daily until the hemorrhoids are reversed

- RaspaMax freeze-dried red and black raspberry powder: T. or more daily

- Beta-caryophyllene-rich supercritical organic cannabis extract plus CO_2 extract of wild turmeric (that is Canacurmin) as mycellized sublingual drops: 10 or more drops twice daily

Irritable bowel syndrome and/or ulcerative colitis

The benefit of raw, unprocessed turmeric extract for all colonic diseases is immense. This is largely a consequence of its antiinflammatory powers as well as its capacity to stimulate the digestive processes. No doubt, the intake of turmeric or its extracts functions as an aid to digestive secretion, particularly the production of bile. Since it curbs inflammation it has a calming action on the bowel wall, easing and/or preventing cramps. This antiinflammatory capacity makes turmeric an ideal adjunct in the treatment of Crohn's disease and ulcerative colitis.

In these syndromes there is digestive impairment. A more thorough digestion and processing of food, which turmeric, as well as ginger, achieves, is instrumental in reversing these conditions. The regular consumption of whole food turmeric and ginger will have a dramatic, positive effect, particularly if combined with the supplement concentrate as 500 mg capsules. In the case of extreme digestive distress the concentrate may be taken as sublingual drops, which achieves direct absorption without entering the gut.

Treatment protocol

- whole food turmeric extract with wild rosemary, wild oregano, and raw ginger extract: 40 drops three times daily or two gelcaps two or three times daily

- whole food, raw, wild turmeric extract with wild rosemary and oregano: two capsules twice daily

- whole food, organic turmeric powder: two tsp. twice daily

- raw, organic turmeric: at least one root daily

- whole food enzyme complex with ginger and cardamom: two or more capsules with meals

- total body purging agent to obliterate compromising parasites: one or two ounces daily

- plant-source problotic formula, that is Ecologic 500: half tsp. or more at night in a glass of luke-warm water

- whole food digestive enzyme complex combined with spice concentrates, that is Gastronex: two or three capsules with each meal

- Beta-caryophyllene-rich supercritical organic cannabis extract plus CO_2 extract of wild turmeric (that is Canacurmin) as mycellized sublingual drops: 10 or more drops twice daily

Chapter Ten

Cleansing and Prevention

For the prevention of human disease spices are essential. In many respects turmeric is the most diverse of all spice preventive agents. It has a prolonged use for detoxification of the body. It also has a primary use for skin disorders. Additionally, it has been relied upon to rebuild the body after it has been stressed or weakened, as in exhaustion syndromes, nutritional deficiency, prostration, recovery from disease, and also anemia. Here, it should be kept in mind that as a root turmeric is highly nutrient dense, just as are carrots, turnips, and potatoes.

Much of its wholesome power, including its cleansing and detoxification actions, relate to its capacity as an antioxidant, evaluated through a system known as ORAC testing. So, let us review this power to gain an appreciation of its immense value for the health of the skin as well as the internal organs.

Why turmeric is ideal

It would appear that in regard to modern humans turmeric has been fully neglected. For local Asian and Indian populations it has been valued for its medicinal properties for centuries. Incredibly, in the United States of all places in the world it is least commonly consumed, and this may be directly related to the extreme vulnerability of Americans to degenerative diseases, particularly arthritis, dementia, multiple sclerosis, Parkinson's disease, fibromyalgia, and Alzheimer's disease.

There is also a great degree of digestive disorders in the Western world, once again, more so than is seen in the Orient. This, too, may be related to low intake of turmeric and other digestion-stimulating spices. Yet, it is much more than a mere stimulant. Turmeric is a powerful detoxification agent for all elements of the digestive tract, including the stomach, intestines, colon, pancreas, liver, and gallbladder. Because of its astringent action it tones the entire gut, boosting the flow also of digestive juices, while also increasing the absorption of nutrients. The tonic action makes it an effective agent against weakness of the stomach and intestines as well as spasticity and hemorrhoids. Its purging and detoxification actions make it an effective antiparasitic agent, and it also aids in the cleansing from the gut of noxious bacteria. Even so, that cleansing action explains its value in skin disorders such as eczema and psoriasis.

Regarding the maintenance of optimal health Americans, in particular, are at a vast loss as a result. Turmeric is effective against dozens of common diseases. In this regard it possesss a wide array of therapeutic activities. These activities may be listed, as follows:

- capacity to induce wound healing
- ability to modulate and control in a positive matter some 600-plus genes
- increase the synthesis of cell survival proteins

- increase the synthesis of genetic matter, that is DNA and RNA
- modulate and minimize inflammatory molecules
- improved blood sugar control through reduction in insulin resistance
- increasing the resistance of cell membranes to oxidation and disease processes
- overall reduction in pro-inflammation molecules

It makes sense that this is the case. It explains why turmeric is so useful for such a diverse range of diseases and conditions. Thus, it is no surprise that, historically, it has been relied upon for digestive complaints, sprains/injuries, skin disorders, joint pain, brain health, and eye function.

Psoriasis/eczema

The positive effects of turmeric in psoriasis and eczema are clear and obvious. This makes sense. Since antiquity the spice has been relied upon for skin disorders, both topically and internally. Chronic skin conditions, such as psoriasis, dermatitis, and eczema, are associated with a significant degree of inflammation. Turmeric and its extracts effectively block this, with great power to do so within the skin and its deeper layers. For fighting skin disorders it should be taken in all the possible forms: the raw and powdered root, along with the raw CO_2 extract. It should also be applied topically in the form of a cream and ointment.

As an internal treatment turmeric works best if taken with wild chaga, the latter being a potent remedy for psoriasis, dermatitis, seborrhea, and eczema. It is raw chaga which is most effective, for instance, as a water-extracted sublingual drops and capsules with wild birch bark and wild oregano. Wild chaga tea, ideally with birch bark, is also somewhat active against such skin conditions.

In some extreme cases it is also necessary to do a parasite purge. Such organisms, particularly intestinal and liver flukes, act as the primary cause, especially in severe cases of full-body psoriasis and eczema. To obliterate these pathogens take the wild-based total body purging agent, containing wild, raw dandelion, nettle, and burdock leaf extracts, an ounce or ideally two ounces every a.m. on an empty stomach. For a more aggressive effect it can even be taken in a dose of two ounces twice daily.

Treatment protocol

- whole food turmeric extract with wild rosemary, wild oregano, and raw ginger extract: 20 drops three times daily or two gelcaps two or three times daily

- whole food, organic and/or wild turmeric powder: two tsp. twice daily

- raw, organic turmeric: at least one root daily

- turmeric-based cream or ointment, either pre-made or homemade: apply as needed, especially at night. Beware of staining, the pigment being difficult to wash out. Note: a simple method of removing turmeric stains is to spray coloration with Germ-a-Clenz, adding Shout or a similar commercial stain remover, scrubbing it in and then letting it sit in the sun. In most instances this will completely remove it.

- wild, raw chaga sublingual drops (Chag-o-Power drops): two squirts twice daily

- raw, wild chaga capsules with wild birch bark: two or more capsules twice daily

- total body purging agent, an ounce or ideally two ounces every a.m. on an empty stomach

- whole food vitamin complex with natural-source vitamin E, B complex, along with vitamins A and D (that is Purely-PAK), one packet daily

- plant-source probiotic formula, that is Ecologic 500: half tsp. or more at night in a glass of luke-warm water

- Beta-caryophyllene-rich supercritical organic cannabis extract plus CO_2 extract of wild turmeric (that is Canacurmin) as mycellized sublingual drops: 10 or more drops twice daily

Toxic overload

The majority of humans are suffering from a significant degree of toxin overload. Historically, turmeric has been used as a "cleansing agent" for the body, deemed a means to "purify" the tissues, including the blood, skin, and internal organs. Yet, it also directly fights toxicity from exposure to a variety of noxious agents. Consider its powers versus chemical steroids. It has a major capacity to reduce steroid toxicity when given simultaneously with the drug. Thus, for all persons taking powerful antiinflammatory agents, not just steroids but also non-steroidal antiinflammatory agents, the intake of turmeric extracts is a must. The same is true of all people who are taking a multiplicity of drugs. There are no untoward reactions of turmeric with pharmaceutical agents and, rather, it appears to cause them to work more effectively.

Moreover, turmeric in all its whole food forms is an ideal overall purging agent, causing the dumping through the stool of every manner of poison and toxin. This includes stored-up levels of noxious petrochemicals in the liver, for instance, residues of pesticides, herbicides, dioxins, PCBs, and bisphenols. With turmeric therapy the stool may have an odd stench as it dumps out that litany of toxins and poisons.

Treatment protocol

- raw, organic turmeric: at least one root daily

- wild, raw turmeric extract as sublingual drops: 20 drops twice daily; for extreme toxicity double or triple this amount

- whole food, raw, wild turmeric extract with wild rosemary and oregano: two capsules twice daily

- wild turmeric powder: one or more tsp. daily either in food or turmeric milk; for extreme toxicity double this amount

- total body purging agent with black seed oil and wild, raw greens extracts: an ounce in the a.m. on an empty stomach for at least two weeks

Hives and itchy skin

As was well established by early civilizations turmeric is highly effective for skin disorders. In this regard it acts as an antiinflammatory agent and also an antihistamine. In Indian culture it is used for a wide range of skin conditions, including hives, psoriasis, eczema, and itchy skin. Regarding the latter it is an effective antipruritic agent, meaning it fights and/or reverses itching. For hives it acts as a powerful antiinflammatory agent, reducing and/or eliminating swelling, redness, and itching. The actions of turmeric are enhanced through the fruit enzymes, bromelain and papain, which are found, along with the spice, in the highly potent enzyme complex, InflamEEZ.

Treatment protocol

- raw, organic turmeric: at least one root daily

- bromelain and papain complex with turmeric and ginger (that is InflamEEZ): two or more capsules on an empty stomach as often as needed to eliminate the symptoms

- wild, raw turmeric extract as sublingual drops: 40 drops twice daily

- whole food, raw, wild turmeric extract with wild rosemary and oregano: one or more capsules twice daily

Vitiligo

Though it is little realized this condition is caused largely by an imbalance in endocrine function, specifically disruptions of the adrenals and pituitary. When these glands suffer in decline, the skin becomes vulnerable to attack, in this case by a melanocyte-eating fungus, pityriasis. With vitiligo it is necessary to normalize the function of the melanocytes, that is the pigment-depositing cells. A number of spices achieve this, notably wild rosemary, wild oregano, and turmeric. Extracts of all such spices are potent anti-vitiligo treatments. Chaga mushroom extract, rich in melanin, is also an effective treatment for this condition. It is also crucial to kill the fungus, which to a degree the turmeric achieves, although the wild oregano is more potent in this regard.

Treatment protocol

- raw, organic turmeric: at least one root daily

- wild, raw turmeric extract as sublingual drops: 40 drops twice daily

- whole food, raw, wild turmeric extract with wild rosemary and oregano: two capsules twice daily

- whole food vitamin complex with natural-source vitamin E, B complex, along with vitamins A and D (that is Purely-PAK), one packet daily

- wild, raw chaga as water-extracted sublingual drops, take 20 to 40 drops under the tongue twice daily

- wild, raw chaga skin cream: apply twice daily

- adrenal support capsules with 3x royal jelly plus rosemary and sage: two or more capsules twice daily

Moles and/or age spots

Moles and age spots are associated with excessive pigment deposition. With age spots there is lipofuscin pigment deposition, which is a toxin associated with excessive aging and free radical damage. Both internally and, topically, turmeric extracts are effective against these lesions. Moreover, regarding reversal of these skin disorders the wild type is the most potent of all. This formula as a mycellized oil can be taken internally but also applied topically. Regarding moles, there are other effective therapies, notably oil of wild oregano and also wild, raw chaga extracts. For age spots whole food vitamin sources are necessary to prevent further development and induce regression. As well, oils of wild myrtle, sage, and rosemary help induce regression of both of these lesions.

Treatment protocol

- raw, organic turmeric: at least one root daily

- whole food, raw, wild turmeric extract with wild rosemary and oregano: one or more capsules twice daily

- whole food vitamin complex with natural-source vitamin E, B complex, along with vitamins A and D (that is Purely-PAK), one packet daily

- wild, raw chaga sublingual drops: 40 drops twice daily

- wild, raw chaga skin cream: apply twice daily

- Beta-caryophyllene-rich supercritical, organic cannabis extract plus CO_2 extract of wild oregano (that is Hempanol): 10 or more drops twice daily

Anemia

It seems incredible but, in fact, spices are among the most effective therapeutic agents known for this condition. This is largely a result of their density of iron and other blood-building minerals. Turmeric is, perhaps, the most iron dense of all spices. This should be no surprise since, historically, it has been relied upon as a primary anti-anemia agent.

The iron content of turmeric is rich beyond belief. Offering some 300% of the daily minimum in a mere 100 grams, in fact, it is so dense that it may be relied upon as an iron supplement for all types of anemia. Plus, it is in an organically bound form, which is far superior and far safer versus the synthetic or chemical forms. The fresh root and the root juice are the most powerful blood builders of all. In the isolate-based supplements virtually all the iron is lost during manufacturing. The exceptions are whole food forms, for instance, Turmeric-PLUS sublingual drops and capsules. Both these supplements are effective for reversing anemia and various disorders associated with low red blood cell counts. For optimal results all the various forms should be used, including the fresh root and/or root juice, along with powdered turmeric spice. Other spices which aid in the building of healthy, normal blood counts include black seed, cumin, wild oregano, and wild sage.

Foods rich in iron must be consumed regularly. Yet, the type of the mineral makes a difference. The iron in liver and eggs is readily absorbed and utilized by the body. Liver contains a number of other blood-building factors, which greatly aid in the regeneration of red blood cells. For both these foods only organic, non-GMO sources must be used.

Treatment protocol

- raw, organic turmeric: at least one root daily

- whole food, raw, wild turmeric extract with wild rosemary and oregano: two capsules twice daily

- wild-source turmeric powdered spice: two tsp. daily

- whole food vitamin complex with natural-source vitamin E, B complex, along with vitamins A and D (that is Purely-PAK), one or more packets daily

- wild oregano crude herb with Rhus coriaria: three capsules twice daily

- crushed black seed plus cumin and red sour grape: two or more capsules twice daily

- lemon juice and spinach salad with chopped turmeric root: consume daily

- organic liver plus two or three eggs over easy: consume at least twice per week

Obesity

The treatment of obesity is one of the most unheralded uses for turmeric, despite its immense effectiveness. To a degree all spices are weight loss agents, largely as a consequence of their capacities as thermogenic agents. Even mustard has this property. Perhaps with the propensity of the Indo-Pakistani population to consume such major amounts of turmeric and mustard, for instance, as in pickled mangoes: perhaps this explains why in their native culture they are so thin.

In all forms turmeric aids weight loss. Thus, for those with weight challenges adding this spice liberally to cooking is a wise approach. The raw root should be routinely consumed in salads. In addition, it can be juiced and the liquor added to smoothies and vegetable juices. The supplement, too, is effective, especially the raw, wild whole food type. As well, turmeric milk is also a weight loss agent, especially when made with ginger and cinnamon, the latter being an effective blood sugar regulating agent.

Treatment protocol

- wild-source turmeric powdered spice: two tsp. daily or consume in turmeric milk, at least one tsp. daily

- raw, organic turmeric: at least one root daily

- whole food, raw, wild turmeric extract with wild rosemary and oregano: two capsules twice daily

- whole food, raw, sacha inchi oil: 2 T. daily in the a.m. as a thermogenic agent

- triple spice-based coconut fat, that is CocaSpice: One T. or more daily taken directly or used in cooking

Radiation toxicity

There are a number of ways the individual can become intoxicated by radiation. A major source is radiation-based therapy for cancer and other diseases. Yet another is exposure to medical X-rays, not just in regard to patients but also doctors and technicians. Today, there is vast radiation exposure as a result of nuclear power plant accidents. This is a far more pervasive source than most people realize. As a result of the more well-published nuclear power plant meltdowns, such as Three Mile Island, Chernobyl, and Fukushima, countless millions of people have been extensively contaminated. Then, too, the number of animals exposed is beyond count, and with Fukushima, all living creatures in the oceans have been extensively contaminated, particularly the inhabitants of the Pacific Ocean west of Japan. There were also additional accidents that were completely disguised where there was no public information available, for instance, the Zion, Illinois, 'partial' meltdown and the Simi Valley nuclear disaster. Regarding the latter it is estimated that the radiation released is some 200-fold greater than all that arising from Three Mile Island. It was completely covered up, thanks to the criminal minds of the US nuclear cabal. No one knows how many people developed cancer from this catastrophe, but it surely numbers in the tens of thousands.

Fukushima is a far more profound debacle than most people realize. The leakage of radioactive ions from nuclear power plants, whether as a result of actual meltdowns or simply from discharges and various 'accidents,' is routinely covered-up. It is a criminal clique which is behind such plants. In this regard it should be realized that there is no actual basis for such plants. The facilities are never profitable and, thus, must be subsidized. Yet, what is the source of those subsidies? It is none other than the fully bamboozled, heavily taxed general public that must suffer under this burden, paying for these subsidies while suffering the consequences of nuclear power plant-related poisoning.

Even if an accident or meltdown is publicized, still, everything is done that is possible to minimize it. There is no official information regarding the poisonous effects of either Chernobyl or Fukushima. Yet, both are continuously poisoning this earth, Fukushima being even more deadly and dangerous than the Russian accident. In particular, people living on the American West Coast are being constantly bombarded with excesses of radiation as a result of the continuous release of radiological ions from this catastrophe. The Pacific Ocean is fully polluted. Virtually all large-size tuna from this ocean are radioactive, testing positive for Fukushima-source cesium.

Medical procedures and diagnostics are a major additional source for radiation exposure. For instance, a single CT-Scan is equivalent to some 100 chest x-rays in total irradiation. There are nuclear procedures for evaluating heart functions based on the radioactive isotope thorium, the latter being injected into the body. For thyroid disorders radioactive iodine is injected for purposes of destroying the gland. Additionally, dental x-rays are no minor source, and now, CT-Scans of the head are applied, which assault the body with massive levels of radioactivity. Along with exposure to excessive solar radiation dental and CT-Scans may well be the most common, insidious cause of the cataract epidemic.

Treatment protocol

- radiation-purging capsules made with bentonite, zeolite, and chlorella, that is Toxi-Purge capsules: two or more capsules twice daily

- wild, raw turmeric CO_2 extract as 500 mg capsules with wild rosemary: one or two capsules twice daily

- wild mycellized turmeric plus rosemary and oregano as sublingual drops: 20 or more drops twice daily

- wild, raw chaga as water soluble sublingual drops: 40 or more drops twice daily

- whole food vitamin C complex: one or two capsules twice daily

- raw, organic turmeric: at least one root daily

- whole food vitamin complex with natural-source vitamin E, B complex, along with vitamins A and D (that is Purely-PAK), one packet daily

Infertility

In Ayurvedic medicine turmeric has been longed used as a fertility aid. It is known to reduce inflammation in the female pelvis, while also aiding in the induction of ovulation. For men it boosts both sperm count and activity, in many cases remarkably so. The most powerful type for this purpose is the whole food extract, along with the dried food-grade spice itself. Also, the raw root and its juice are powerful fertility aids. All these forms contain the hormone-like molecules, the plant sterols, which boost the fertility response. Infertility may be caused by fungal overload, particularly by invasive forms of candida. Thus, to restore a normal capacity to become pregnant and bear children, the yeast must be purged. The purging agent for this is wild oil of oregano, which is a component of the Turmeric-PLUS capsules. Royal jelly also aids in regenerating fertility. This is because it provides a dense amount of sex hormone-like steroids, which help resolve infertility.

Treatment protocol

- whole food turmeric extract with wild rosemary, wild oregano, and raw ginger extract: 20 drops three times daily or two gelcaps two or three times daily

- oil of wild oregano, edible type, daily use: five or more drops under the tongue twice daily

- whole food, organic and/or wild turmeric powder: two tsp. twice daily

- raw, organic turmeric: at least one root daily

- wild, raw turmeric CO_2 extract as 500 mg capsules with wild rosemary: one or two capsules twice daily

- whole food vitamin complex with natural-source vitamin E, B complex, along with vitamins A and D (that is Purely-PAK), one packet daily

- 3x royal jelly with wild rosemary and sage: two capsules twice daily

Eye inflammation and irritation

Another little realized capacity of turmeric is in regard to eye disorders, where it has a rich history of use. Now, it is known that this positive action is largely a function of its antioxidant capacity. Studies have shown that it is effective in the treatment of rather severe eye disorders, including cataracts, retinitis pigmentosa, and macular degeneration. It is of immense utility for inflammatory disorders of these organs, notably uveitis, iritis, and generalized eye irritation. All forms of turmeric have these powers, including the fresh juice, which may be used as an eye wash.

Treatment protocol

- whole food, organic and/or wild turmeric powder: two tsp. twice daily

- raw, organic turmeric: at least one root daily

- wild mycellized turmeric plus rosemary and oregano as sublingual drops: 20 or more drops under the tongue twice daily

- whole food vitamin complex with natural-source vitamin E, B complex, along with vitamins A and D (that is Purely-PAK), one packet daily

- wild, raw turmeric CO_2 extract as 500 mg capsules with wild rosemary: one or two capsules twice daily

- Beta-caryophyllene-rich supercritical organic cannabis extract plus CO_2 extract of wild turmeric (that is Canacurmin) as mycellized sublingual drops: 10 or more drops twice daily

Cataracts

As mentioned previously one of the primary causes of this condition is oxidative damage in the lens. This oxidation may arise from toxic stress. It may also be the result of excessive exposure to sunlight. Radiation injury to the eyes is far more common than is realized. It is surely ultra-common in those receiving X-irradiation therapy as a result of medical therapies and also diagnostic procedures.

Turmeric is a generalized medicine for the eyes. For cataracts it acts by causing an increase in the production of glutathione-S-transferase in the lens epithelium. A water decoction can be made from organic turmeric powder, 1:20, and used to treat infection and/or irritation in the eye. Since antiquity it has been known that this spice helps maintain the shape and integrity of the human eye. It also helps relieve eye pain. Furthermore, in high doses taken internally it may act to prevent the onset of cataracts and/or to block their worsening. In particular, the sublingual drops of the raw, wild turmeric extract is ideal, as this is the means to gain immediate increased blood levels.

Treatment protocol

- whole food turmeric extract with wild rosemary, wild oregano, and raw ginger extract: 10 or more drops under the tongue two or three times daily or two gelcaps two or three times daily

- wild, raw turmeric CO_2 extract as 500 mg capsules with wild rosemary: one or two capsules twice daily

- whole food, organic turmeric powder: two tsp. twice daily

- raw, organic turmeric: at least one root daily

- whole food vitamin complex with natural-source vitamin E, B complex, along with vitamins A and D (that is Purely-PAK), one packet daily

- wild rosemary essence plus essence of rose blossoms; make a 50/50 mixture of these waters and use in an eye cup twice daily

Chapter Eleven

Recipes and Remedies

When it is about health, it is time to cook with spices. Yet, in the Western world the extensive use of the spice cabinet is uncommon. Regarding turmeric, it is rarely added to cooking and is reserved to, essentially, special trips to the Indian or Middle Eastern restaurant.

Then, how is the unfamiliar person to use this spice? Ideally, it should be cooked in any fat-based dishes, since it blends readily in fatty compounds to unleash both its rich flavors and therapeutic properties.

With cooking a person can enjoy this spice, while gaining immense benefits. Moreover, all its forms can and should be used. The fresh root can now be bought in many specialty stores and also in major chains. Care should be taken with it. The root must be stored properly. To do so it must be layered in air-tight containers, with a dry paper towel between layers. In this way it will last up to a month without molding. Kept refrigerated, it should be checked for dampness of the paper towels, which must be replaced. Alternatively, a few drops of oil of wild oregano can be rubbed about the container to block mold growth and lengthen preservation.

For cooking the root should be peeled and to prevent the most loss using a potato peeler. A goodly amount can be pre-peeled for later use in cooking. It may also be minced or presliced, readied for adding to recipes and smoothies. Finely grated turmeric, notes Chef Jennifer Iserloh, can be added to all varieties of beverages, including hot teas, coffee drinks, and tart juices, like grapefruit juice and unsweetened cranberry juice. It also makes a great addition to, in particular, carrot juice, along with fresh ginger.

Turmeric blends well with a wide range of other spices. This is its infamous use, for instance, as a primary ingredient of that multi-spice complex, curry powder. There is much talk about blending it with black pepper, which is traditional. This is largely because of published research demonstrating a particular action of black pepper on turmeric absorption. Notably, a special compound in this spice, piperine, facilitates absorption of key turmeric compounds, particularly the pigment curcumin. Heavy use, though, of black pepper is not emphasized, here, because the spice can be irritating to some people. Also, allergy to black pepper is relatively common. Therefore, it can be used with discretion. Those who do well with it can add it to their turmeric recipes as a flavoring and assimilation aid, including sprinkling it into turmeric milk recipes. The emphasis in this book is on the addition of ginger and its extracts, which also facilitate absorption, while being less irritating to the system than black pepper. Even so, for those who tolerate it this spice is traditionally used and can also facilitate the utilization of turmeric active ingredients.

So, enjoy turmeric in all its forms, and gain the most optimal health achievable. Consume it by itself as the lead spice or in combination with its fellow flavors: ginger, cinnamon, curry leaves, black pepper, fennel, and more: bon appétit.

Entrees

Turmeric Omelet

3 organic or free-range eggs, cracked and contents put into bowl
tsp. organic, non-irradiated turmeric powder
3 T. raw onion, minced
2 medium cloves garlic, finely minced
2 T. red sweet pepper or green pepper, minced
butter, ghee, or CocaSpice blend (for extra spice power)
sea salt to taste
freshly ground black pepper to taste (optional)

Whip eggs with salt, pepper, and turmeric until well blended. On medium-low heat in a coated skillet heat fat and add onions, garlic, and peppers; cook until just tender, then pour over egg-spice mixture. Cook until firm enough to either flip or turn over in half, cooking until reaching desired doneness.

Simple CocaSpice Fried Rice

½ cup leftover cooked brown rice
½ cup leftover cooked wild rice, (if unavailable, replace with 1/2 cup brown rice)
3 T. CocaSpice aromatic coconut oil
½ red onion, minced
3 organic eggs, slightly scrambled (optional)
3 spears broccoli, minced
4 garlic cloves, minced
½ green pepper, chopped
2 tsp. organic turmeric powder
sea salt to taste

In a skillet or wok heat oil on medium or medium-high heat and cook onions, garlic, green pepper, and broccoli until tender, adding turmeric and salt until well blended. Set aside. In a skillet or wok cook left-over cooked rice in remaining oil, adding extra salt, until hot throughout. Add eggs and vegetable mixture; continue cooking until piping hot and rice becomes slightly crisp. Serve with full fat yogurt topping, if desired.

CocaSpice-Cooked Lamb Burgers with Diced Onions and Broccoli Bits

2 T. or more CocaSpice
1 lb. organic ground lamb
1 medium onion, diced
tsp. HerbSorb powder (Americanwildfoods.com) or Herbamere (optional)
2 medium stalks broccoli, finely minced
sea salt to taste (used only after the meat is done)

There are two ways to prepare this. The onions and broccoli can either be mixed into the raw meat patties or cooked separately and then poured over. For cooking separately in a skillet brown the vegetable/onion in a T. of CocaSpice until soft; set aside. Mix HerbSorb or Herbamere into the meat and make four to six patties. Cook lamb patties to desired doneness, while reheating the broccoli-onion mixture and add on as garnish. The second option is to mix all the contents together and cook the patties in 1 or 2 T. CocaSpice.

Wild Salmon in Turmeric-Coconut Sauce with Sliced Onions

1 pound wild salmon cut into four filets
one medium onion, sliced
fine sea salt
freshly ground black pepper
3 T. CocaSpice oil
red sour grape powder (that is Resvital powder) or use lemon juice, if
    unavailable

Cook onions until soft in olive oil or coconut oil (or CocaSpice); set aside.

Season salmon with red sour grape (or lemon juice), sea salt, and black pepper. In a large skillet on medium-high heat cook salmon in CocaSpice oil, skin side down, undisturbed, until skin is crisped and browned (about three to four minutes). Turn fillet and cook until just opaque at center, about one or two minutes for medium-rare. Dress with onions and pour any remaining spice oil over the top and serve.

Indian-Style Mango Dal

When this recipe, adapted from the menu of EatingWell.com, is served over brown rice, it makes a full meal as a vegetarian entree. Use it for this purpose or serve it as an accent to a high-protein or meat-based entrée.

1 cup yellow lentils
4 cups filtered water
1 tsp. sea salt, divided
1 tsp. ground turmeric
1 T. cold-pressed sesame oil (ideally, Sesam-E) or, preferably, CocaSpice
    oil (optional: red palm oil may be used)
½ tsp. cumin seeds
½ tsp. ground coriander
¼ tsp. cayenne pepper powder
1 T. minced fresh ginger
2 organic mangoes, peeled and diced
1 medium yellow onion, diced
3 cloves garlic, minced
½ cup chopped fresh cilantro

In a colander place lentils and rinse well. In a large saucepan combine with four cups water, ½ tsp. sea salt, and turmeric and bring to a boil. Reduce heat to simmer, partially cover, and cook, stirring occasionally: about 14 minutes. Meanwhile, in a large nonstick skillet heat oil over medium heat, adding cumin seeds and cooking until fragrant and starting to brown: about 30 seconds. Add onion; cook, stirring, until soft and beginning to brown: about 5 minutes. Add garlic, ginger, coriander, cayenne, and the remaining salt and cook, stirring for one minute more. Add in garlic mixture plus mangoes and lentils. Return to a simmer and cook, stirring occasionally until they are falling apart: about 11 to 15 minutes. Stir in cilantro and serve over brown rice, if desired.

Fast-Style Chicken Masala for Two

Adapted from recipe published on www.eatingwell.com

2 tsp. garam masala

1 tsp. organic turmeric powder

½ tsp. sea salt

contents 2 OregaMax capsules (optional)

¼ cup finely milled wheat flour (if gluten intolerant, use brown rice flour)

8 ounces organic chicken tenders

T. CocaSpice oil or organic sesame oil, divided

2 cloves garlic, minced

2 tsp. minced fresh ginger

1 fifteen oz. can diced tomatoes, undrained

2 T. organic or natural whipping cream

¼ cup chopped, fresh cilantro

In a small dish mix spices, garam masala, turmeric, contents of OregaMax, and salt. In a shallow dish or firm paper plate place flour. Sprinkle chicken with a half teaspoon or so of spice mixture, then dredge in flour (reserve the remaining spice mix and flour). Heat a teaspoon of oil in a skillet over medium-high heat. Cook chicken until browned: about 2 minutes each side. Transfer to a plate.

Heat remaining oil in pan over medium-low heat, adding garlic, onion, ginger, and cook, stirring often, about 4 minutes. Then, add the rest of the spice mix and cook, stirring until fragrant, about a minute. Sprinkle with reserved flour and stir until well coated. Add tomatoes and their juice and bring to a simmer, cooking, while stirring often: about another 4 to 5 minutes. Stir in whipping cream, then add chicken plus any accumulated spices to the pan. Bring to a simmer, and cook over medium-low heat until chicken is fully cooked: another 4 minutes. Garnish with cilantro.

Spiced Eggs Over Easy

3 organic or free-range eggs, cracked and poured gently into bowl

½ tsp. organic turmeric powder

contents of 3 OregaMax capsules (optional)

dash or two cayenne pepper
freshly ground black pepper
1 T. CocaSpice oil or, if unavailable, organic butter

In a coated skillet heat oil on medium heat, adding eggs when oil is hot. Dust with spices, then turn gently and dust with remaining spices, cooking gently, keeping yolk liquid. Use of CocaSpice is ideal, being rich in wild, organic turmeric, as it imparts a delicious, luscious taste.

Pan-Fried Indian Shrimp

1 pound raw shrimp, peeled and deveined with tails left on
½ tsp. sea salt
½ tsp. cayenne pepper
½ tsp. organic turmeric powder
2 T. extra virgin olive oil or CocaSpice
1 bunch green tops of scallions, thinly sliced
¼ cup parsley, finely diced
2 T. green pepper, diced

Toss shrimp with spices and salt in medium bowl. Cover and refrigerate for 30 minutes. In a large non-stick skillet over medium-high heat add oil and heat, placing shrimp in single layer, cooking until undersides turns pinkish: about one minute. Flip over and cook for another minute. Add scallions and parsley, along with green pepper and continue cooking, gently stirring, until shrimp s just fully done and starts to begin to curl: about 2 minutes. Serve hot with shrimp sauce or as topping for salad.

Kale-Enriched Scrambled Turmeric Eggs

This is one of the most nutritious recipes possible, combining two nutrient-dense foods, kale and eggs plus virgin coconut oil. It's the flavor imparted by that special spice emulsion oil, CocaSpice, combined with a bit of cayenne, which gives this is its supremely luscious flavor.

3 organic or free range eggs, cracked and lightly whipped
2 medium stalks organic kale, well washed, shredded

a good size chunk, red onion
½ tsp. organic or non-irradiated turmeric powder
1 T. CocaSpice oil
sea salt to taste
dash or two cayenne pepper

In a skillet on medium temperature heat oil, adding onion and kale, then stirring in turmeric until well blended with the kale and onions. Let cook until kale and onions are tender. Add eggs plus some salt and dash or two of cayenne. Cook to desired doneness but do not overcook, as this will diminish the rich flavor.

Healthy Turmeric Chicken Stew

2 T. extra virgin olive oil or CocaSpice oil
2 skinless, boneless organic chicken breasts, cubed
2 medium sweet potatoes, sliced and halved
½ red onion, chopped
1 small eggplant, cubed
3 cloves garlic, minced
2 tsp. ground turmeric
1 T minced fresh ginger root
½ cup organic chicken broth
2 T. diced red sweet pepper
4 organic button mushrooms, diced

In a large skillet heat oil over medium-high heat. Add chicken; cook until browned and no longer pink in center: about 5 minutes. Add sweet potatoes and onion; cook until onion is soft: about 3 minutes. Add eggplant, garlic, red pepper, ginger, and turmeric; cook until fragrant, about 1 minute more. Add broth; simmer until thickened, stirring occasionally: about 20 minutes.

Spicy Turmeric Beef

adapted from a recipe by mykitchensnippets.com
1lb organic beef tenderloin, thinly sliced

purified water, enough to cover the beef

4 T. CocaSpice oil

2 small potatoes, peeled and cut into 1-inch pieces, par-boiled until
  slightly soft

1 T. organic turmeric powder

3 cloves garlic, chopped

1 red or yellow pepper, coarsely chopped

2 red chilies cut small

½ red onion, coarsely diced

sea salt and black pepper to taste

In a sauté pan or wok put beef and add water, enough to cover the beef. Cook until soft and water completely evaporates. Stir occasionally. Melt oil in a separate pan stirring in turmeric until well mixed. Pour over beef and add garlic, potato, and turmeric powder. Turn down the flame, stir regularly until the beef looks crunchy and the potato is soft. Add bell peppers, onion as well as salt and pepper to taste. Continue stirring for 2 minutes. Serve with hot brown rice.

Vegetable Dishes

Brussels Sprouts in Yogurt-Turmeric Sauce

24 Brussels sprouts, outer tough or discolored leaves peeled, hard stems removed

½ or more cup extra virgin olive oil

1½ cups plain whole organic yogurt

2 tsp. organic turmeric powder

five to ten drops Turmeric-Plus extract (optional)

2 tsp. ground cumin

1 tsp. ground coriander

T. or more sea salt

Wash Brussels sprouts well. Then, slice them in bite-sized slices. In a large skilled add oil. Heat and add Brussels sprouts; cook until partially done, about five minutes. Stir in yogurt, salt, cumin, turmeric, and coriander. Cook for five or more minutes or until oil glistens, making sure the spices are fully combined with the vegetable. Heat for another few minutes and serve.

Why use turmeric more commonly? It is more than just for taste. Being a root turmeric is unusually nutritionally dense. it is a top source of a number of key nutrients, particularly the minerals manganese and iron. It is also relatively dense in vitamin B-6, offering some 4% of the daily requirement in a mere 2 teaspoons.

Oven-Cooked Tandoori-Coconut Root Vegetables

Adapted from a recipe by Claire Saffitz on www.bonappetit.com

half bunch of medium-sized to small carrots, cleaned, peeled, or scraped
half bunch medium-sized to small parsley roots, cleaned, peeled, or scraped
half bunch of small parsnip roots, cleaned, peeled, or scraped
2 tsp. organic turmeric powder
½ tsp. organic cinnamon powder
2 tsp. dried onions
sea salt
freshly ground black pepper
6 T. CocaSpice
3 large cloves garlic, grated
3 T. freshly squeezed lemon juice
½ cup full fat yogurt
4 T. very coarsely chopped parsley leaves
several wedges of lemon
2 tsp. red sour grape powder (optional)

Preheat oven to 425 degrees. In a small skillet on very low heat 4 T. CocaSpice until warm and just melted, stirring in half the garlic, 1/4 cup yogurt, along with salt and pepper. Add root vegetables; toss and coat. Place root vegetables on baking tray; roast in a single layer, turning occasionally until tender, about 25 to 30 minutes.

Heat turmeric and remaining CocaSpice over medium heat in a small skillet, swirling, about 2 minutes, then remove from heat. In a small bowl whisk in red sour grape (if available) and lemon juice, along with remaining yogurt and garlic, seasoning with extra salt and pepper.

On a platter place all root veggies and drizzle with yogurt-oil mixture. Severe with lemon wedges.

Fenneled Green Cabbage in Turmeric-Yogurt Sauce

1 head green cabbage, cut in 1-inch x 1-inch x 3-inch chunks
½ cup CocaSpice oil
1 tsp. asafoetida
1 T. fennel seed (or fennel seed powder, if unavailable)
1 T. sea salt
2 tsp. organic turmeric powder
1 T. ground coriander

Place cabbage pieces in a colander; rinse thoroughly. Drain completely and pat dry. In a large skillet heat oil on medium-high heat for about a minute, adding asafoetida, allowing it to sizzle for a few seconds. After five minutes add yogurt, stirring continuously for at least one minute, then add salt, coriander, fennel, and turmeric. Cook for about five minute and serve. Refrigerate remainder and serve within 48 hours, as dish tends to lose texture.

Carrot and Onion Curry

This is a tasty side-dish and quick to prepare. Carrots are highly nourishing to the body and are also anti-cancer, being high in beta carotene and other anti-tumor pigments.

½ pound carrots, peeled and cut in chunks
2 medium onions, chunked
3 cloves garlic, diced

3 T. CocaSpice
sea salt to taste
2 tsp. organic turmeric powder

In a skillet heat CocaSpice oil with added turmeric powder, and cook carrots, garlic, and onions until tender. Serve ideally with a meat or fish entree.

Salads and Soups

Spinach-Turmeric Blood-Building Salad

bunch of fresh organic spinach or baby spinach leaves
3 T. freshly squeezed lemon juice
2 T. extra virgin olive oil
one medium clove garlic, minced (optional)
chunk red sweet pepper, minced (for color and taste)
one turmeric root chunk, outer skin peeled or scraped off, cut in small slices
sea salt to taste

Wash thoroughly and de-stem spinach if using bunch of leaves and place sufficient leaves for a salad in a medium bowl, adding minced red pepper. In a small container add lemon juice, olive oil, garlic, turmeric, and salt to taste. Toss with lemon and oil mixture and serve.

Roasted Broccoli 'n Turmeric Salad

5 stalks organic broccoli, lower hard stems removed, well washed
2 cups chopped Lacinato kale (or baby kale)
1 large red sweet pepper, cored, seeded, and sliced
1 cup cooked garbanzo beans
2 or 3 T. organic golden raisins
1 T. extra virgin olive oil
1 tsp. sea salt
freshly crushed black pepper to taste

a dash or two cayenne pepper (optional)
2 tsp. Mediterranean pomegranate syrup (that is PomaMax)

Turmeric Dressing
3 T. extra virgin olive oil
2 T. raw apple cider vinegar
2 T. raw honey
1 tsp. organic or wild turmeric
1 tsp. yellow curry powder
½ tsp. kosher salt
cracked pepper
2 cloves garlic, minced
contents of two OregaMax capsules (optional)

Cut broccoli into florettes and place in bowl, tossing with olive oil and ½ teaspoon salt and a few twists of cracked pepper. Mix well and place on a parchment lined baking sheet. In an oven preheated to 400 and roast broccoli and red swee peppers for about 35 to 40 minutes or until tender, stirring once or twice. In a large bowl place kale, garbanzos, and raisins.

To make the dressing combine all dressing ingredients in a small bowl. Once broccoli is fork tender, add to bowl, mixing with kale and garbanzos. Pour dressing over and mix until combined.

Curried Cold-Weather Soup

1 medium onion, chopped
2 cloves garlic, crushed
1½ tsp. curry powder
1¼ tsp. organic turmeric powder
tsp. cumin seed powder or HerbSorb spice mix (see www.americanwildfoods.com)
8 cups vegetable stock
1 cup frozen organic peas
1 28-oz. can organic diced tomatoes
¼ cup uncooked brown rice
1 medium spaghetti squash

¼ cup dried lentils
sea salt to taste
olive oil, as needed
CocaSpice aromatic cooking oil (an ideal option to olive oil for sautéing)

Cut squash in half, and place cut side down on lightly oiled baking pan, baking at 350 degrees for at least 30 minutes. Remove and set aside to cool, so it can be handled. With a fork shred squash. In a large soup pot or kettle saute onions and garlic, adding cumin, curry powder, and turmeric, in either olive oil or CocaSpice, cooking until transparent. Add stock and lentils, bringing to a boil. Reduce heat to simmer, then adding chopped tomatoes (and the juice in the can). After 10 minutes add rice and peas. After another 30 minutes or so add spaghetti squash. Simmer until rice is well cooked and serve.

Turmeric and Creamed Broccoli Soup

1 T. organic virgin olive oil or CocaSpice oil
1 small white onion, diced
1 stalk celery, diced
1½ tsp. sea salt
1 tsp. turmeric powder
2 cloves garlic, minced
1 large head organic broccoli, stems removed and cut into florets
5 cups organic vegetable stock
¼ tsp. grated ginger
freshly ground black pepper to taste
cayenne pepper to taste
1 medium avocado
½ fresh lemon or lime
cilantro leaves as garnish

In a large pot with a lid melt oil over medium heat. Add onions and celery, sprinkling with a teaspoon of salt. Cook until soft. Add garlic and tumeric, and continue cooking on low heat while stirring often to keep garlic and turmeric from burning. Add broccoli, vegetable stock ginger, cayenne, black pepper and remaining salt. Cover and cook over medium-low heat until broccoli is tender: about 25 to 30 minutes. Remove from heat and add avocado, cut in slices. Puree soup with an immersion blender until smooth. It can also be blended in a blender, adding more salt, as needed. Pour into soup bowls, topped with cilantro leaves and serve.

Carrot 'n Ginger Turmeric Soup

2 T. organic butter or CocaSpice oil
1 red onion, roughly chopped
1½ pounds carrots, chopped coarsely
2 sticks celery, chopped
1½ tsp. organic turmeric
2 cloves garlic, minced
2-inch piece of ginger, peeled and grated
1 liter organic vegetable stock
dash or two cayenne pepper

As a garnish:
handful cilantro leaves, chopped
3 spring onions, sliced
1 green chili, diced
T. parsley, chopped
4 tsp. organic sesame oil
2 tsp. lime juice

In a large pan over medium heat melt butter or CocaSpice, adding onion, carrot, and celery, cooking for up to 12 minutes, stirring frequently. Add ginger, turmeric , and garlic, mixing well, cooking for an additional five minutes. Pour over the stock; bring to a boil. Reduce heat and simmer for 15 minutes until carrots are just tender. Allow soup to cool a bit and then in batches in a food processor blitz until completely smooth. Return to heat and warm through. In a small bowl combine the ingredients for the garnish. Ladle the soup into the bowls, add to each garnish, as desired.

Coconut Curried Cauliflower Soup

2 T. extra virgin coconut oil

2 medium yellow onions, chopped
1 tsp. sea salt
1 head cauliflower, trimmed and cut into florets
4 ½ cups low-sodium vegetable broth; or, water with one vegan veggie
   cube added, the cube cut into small chunks
1 tsp. ground turmeric
¼ tsp. freshly ground black pepper
1¼ tsp. ground cumin
½ tsp. ground coriander

¼ cup finely minced parsley or cilantro leaves (for garnish)
1 cup coconut milk
a few pinches of cayenne pepper

In a large pot over medium heat warm oil until shimmering. Cook onions, adding ¼ tsp. sea salt until soft (8 or so minutes). Reduce heat and add cauliflower, broth or water, spices, and remaining salt. Over medium-high heat bring to a boil, then reduce to low. Simmer until cauliflower is tender, about 15 minutes.

In a blender in modest batches puree the soup until smooth, then return to soup pot. Stir in the coconut milk and warm, adding additional cayenne or other spices, as desired.

Chinese Cabbage Turmeric Salad

one cup Chinese cabbage, shredded
one-inch section raw turmeric, shredded
1/4 cup daikon radish, shredded

Dressing
2 T. rice or plum vinegar
2 T. cold-pressed sesame oil
¼ tsp. turmeric powder
tsp. Japanese mustard (use plain yellow mustard, if unavailable)
sea salt to taste

Toss salad ingredients until well mixed. Mix the dressing; blend in evenly and serve.

Teas, Smoothies, and Milks

Turmeric Night-Cap

Cow's milk, if tolerated, is a superior sedative over nut milks. So, this makes an ideal beverage for restlessness or insomnia. For those who can handle the spiciness the turmeric dose can be raised to a full teaspoon.

one cup organic or raw milk

¾ tsp. organic turmeric powder

¼ tsp. cinnamon powder

tsp. or two raw honey

Heat milk and blend in spices; stir until well mixed, bringing the milk to a soft boil, then simmer for three to four minutes, adding honey after done. Sip on slowly to gain the optimal benefits.

Turmeric Milk, Japanese Style

(adapted from a recipe by YouTuber, Ela Gale)
This is a common drink in Japan, and it is held to be a valuable adjunct for the prevention of aging, including age-related cognitive decline.

¾ cup warm water

half cup coconut or almond milk

1 tsp. organic turmeric powder (for extra-potent drink add an additional half tsp.)

1 tsp. cinnamon powder; for added potency add five drops Cinnamol CO_2 extract (or, use this instead of the powdered cinnamon, ten drops)

½ tsp. powdered nutmeg

½ tsp. powdered ginger (optional)

stevia or raw honey to desired sweetness

Blend in a blender to mix and then heat gently, serving as a hot tea. Or, cool and serve chilled.

Spicy and Smooth Turmeric-Ginger Smoothie

one orange, peeled and pith removed
½ cup frozen mango chunks
¼ cup frozen pineapple chunks
¾ cup coconut water
1 T. shelled, raw hemp seeds
1 tsp. finely grated, peeled ginger
1½ tsp. peeled, finely grated turmeric
pinch cayenne pepper
two or three pinches sea salt

Using smoothie setting puree orange, mango, pineapple, coconut water, and spices, adding a half cup or so of ice until smooth.

Antiinflammation Turmeric Tonic Supreme
(adapted from a recipe by wholefoodsexplorer.com)

2 whole lemons with white pulp, outer peel cut away
1 whole apple, cored
6 medium pieces organic turmeric or one tsp. organic turmeric powder
    per 8 oz.
one or two one inch chunks ginger
6 sprigs mint
two or three ounces coconut water (to cut taste, if desired)

Put all ingredients in a juicer and juice. Serve over ice. Do not spill on cloths or clothes. Causes difficult-to-remove stains.

Traditional Pakistani Turmeric Drink

8 oz. raw or whole organic milk
½ tsp. or more organic turmeric powder

1 T. ground almonds
1 T. or two raw honey
dash or two cinnamon

Heat milk, stirring in turmeric and almonds; cook on low heat until just begins to boil, then reduce heat, adding honey. Serve immediately, topped with cinnamon.

Turmeric-Almond-Banana Milkshake

1 cup canned whole food coconut milk
½ cup almond milk
1-2 frozen bananas
2 tsp. ground turmeric
1 T. almond butter
¼ cup shredded unsweetened coconut
2 T. NutraHemp vanilla protein powder (if unavailable, use organic whey
    protein powder)
¼ tsp. vanilla extract
pinch or two sea salt or Himalayan salt, or to taste
pinch or two nutmeg, optional

Using a high-speed blender, combine all ingredients until smooth. Serve as is or chill and serve extra-thick.

Hot and Spicy Turmeric Milk
This recipe is adapted from an Internet recipe by Wellness Mama.

2 cups almond, hemp, or hazelnut milk
1 tsp. organic turmeric
½ tsp. organic cinnamon
2 tsp. raw honey or maple syrup or to taste (optional)
two or three pinches of black pepper
chunk of fresh ginger root, peeled or ½ tsp. ginger powder
Pinch or two cayenne pepper

In a high-speed blender blend all ingredients until smooth. Pour into a small sauce pan and heat for 3-5 minutes over medium heat until hot but not boiling. Drink immediately.

Coconut Milk Iced Turmeric Latte

1 cup coconut milk
1 tsp. or two coconut or palm sugar`1 ttsp. finely grated ginger
4 tsp. finely grated, peeled turmeric
1 tsp. or two fresh lemon or lime juice
2 pinches ground cardamom
2 pinches of extra ginger powder
pinch flaky sea salt

In a small bowl whisk coconut milk, turmeric, ginger, lemon juice, and cardamom; after sugar and salt are dissolved, let sit for 10 minutes to let flavors blend. Through a fine mesh sieve strain into a cup, pressing on solids to extract juices. After filling glass with ice, pour over. Top with a dusting of extra cardamom and ginger powder.

Anti-Inflammatory Turmeric Golden Milk

1 T. grated fresh turmeric root (or 2 tsp.s dried ground turmeric powder)
1 tsp. freshly grated ginger root (or ¼ tsp. dried ginger powder)
1 T. coconut oil or ghee
1 tsp. black peppercorns or freshly ground black pepper*
2 cups unsweetened non-dairy milk (homemade almond or cashew milk
    or full-fat coconut)
raw honey or maple syrup, to taste
Other optional additions: ground cinnamon, fresh or ground cardamom,
    and/or vanilla bean

Add the fresh turmeric, ginger, oil or ghee and peppercorns to a mortar and pestle. You can also use a small food processor or blender. Grind until you create a fine, smooth and creamy paste.

Add the milk of your choice to a medium saucepan. I usually use half coconut milk (the canned kind) and half homemade almond milk. You can use whatever you prefer. Add the turmeric ginger paste. Whisk well to combine. Bring mixture to a low and gentle boil, reduce the heat to barely a simmer and allow it to simmer for 5 minutes. Stirring often. Remove from the heat and sweetened to taste with raw honey (or maple syrup). I use about 1 tablespoon local raw honey. Strain the mixture to a fine mesh sieve, if you want it smooth. I rarely bother. Serve warm. Enjoy.

Triple Spiced Wild Oregano Honey

8 to 10 oz. wild oregano honey
4 tsp. wild or organic turmeric
2 tsp. Ceylon-type cinnamon powder
1 tsp. ginger powder
a few pinches cardamom (optional)

Whip spices into honey thoroughly and use as flavoring or delicious addition to golden/turmeric milk. It's delicious on gluten-free toast.

Turmeric-Coconut Latte

½ tsp. organic turmeric
1 cup organic or sulfite-free coconut milk
¼ tsp. ground cinnamon
two or three pinches ground ginger
1 tsp. ghee

Heat coconut milk and spices together until it just boils, then reduce the heat and simmer for three or four minute to let flavors meld, then add ghee, stir until melted, and serve.

Ginger-Turmeric-Cinnamon Wild Honey Flavoring

8 ounces wild oregano honey (or other wild honey)
2 T. organic ginger powder, depending on how strong you prefer
2 T. organic ground turmeric
2 T. organic ground cinnamon

1 organic lemon, grated (for zest, optional)

In a bowl mix all ingredients well. Use as a flavoring for teas or on its own.

Golden Paste Triple Spice Starter for Turmeric Milk

For the perfect cup of turmeric milk Golden paste is ideal. It's the starter that can be reserve for easy use. A super-starter is made from turmeric, ginger, and black pepper blended into a coconut oil base. A sweet starter includes cinnamon instead of black pepper. This is available pre-made under the brand, CocaSpice.

Golden Paste Mix

½ cup organic and/or wild turmeric powder or, preferably, turmeric drink pre-mix (TurmaMilk Mix)
1 cup water
1½ tsp. black pepper
5 T. virgin coconut oil or 4 T. CocaSpice oil

In a stainless steel pot, cook the water, turmeric, and black pepper until it forms a thick paste, stirring and cooking for about 7 to 10 minutes. Remove from heat and add virgin coconut oil, using a whisk to fully mix in the coconut oil or for an enriched flavor, CocaSpice oil. Transfer Golden Paste into a glass jar with a lid, and store in the refrigerator for up to two weeks. Use it to make your own turmeric milk on demand. Though modified, the original recipe was developed by Doug English, a veterinarian who has used turmeric therapeutically in animals ranging from dogs to cats to exotic types, like pet alpacas and even crocodiles.

UPDATE Try Quicker Alternative Method: If you have a high speed blender that heats, like certain models of Vitamix, ThermaMax, or Blendtec, add all of the ingredients to the blender, run on high until heated and well blended, anywhere from 3-6 minutes.

Golden Milk Based on Golden Paste

1 tsp. home-made Golden Paste
2 cups coconut milk or almond milk
raw honey
pinch cinnamon and nutmeg, if desired

In a stainless steel pot, gently heat, but do not boil, 2 cups of milk with 1 tsp. of golden paste. A whisk is helpful to fully mix the paste into the milk. Add optional vanilla, honey (or stevia).

Note: Golden paste can be made in advance and simply stored in the refrigerator. Lasts about two weeks.

Turmeric-Tamarind Tea

inch or two chopped turmeric root
inch chopped ginger root
1 T. fresh tamarind paste
raw honey to taste
2 cups coconut milk

In boiled water add chopped roots and tamarind paste. Let steep. When full of flavor, add raw honey and coconut milk. Reheat to serve warm.

Turmeric-Coconut Milk Tea

2 cups coconut milk
2 or 3 tsp. TurmaMilk Mix
¼ tsp. cloves
¼ tsp. nutmeg
pinch or two of black pepper (optional)
2 T. raw, unprocessed honey or turmeric-wild oregano honey or 2 tsp. yacon syrup

In a saucepan over low heat warm milk, along with all spices and raw honey, while stirring well. Serve and enjoy. Makes two servings. Pour into two cups and enjoy!

Cold Weather-Fighting Turmeric Tea

This recipe is courtesy of Ayurvedic practitioner, C. Vargas, Dallas, Texas

one cup almond or coconut milk
½-inch wide round slice of raw ginger root, peeled and finely chopped
1 tsp. organic turmeric powder
½ tsp. cinnamon powder
½ tsp. cardamom powder
½ tsp. ghee
1 tsp. wild oregano plus organic turmeric, cinnamon, and ginger honey
    (or use any other raw honey)

In a small saucepan gently warm milk; whisk in spices and ghee until there are no lumps. Strain and add honey: enjoy

Chapter 13

Conclusion

Turmeric is one of the creative power's most sophisticated natural medicines. No drug can compare to its scope and capacities. Unlike any known drug it reverses a plethora of diseases without the slightest side effects. In fact, it's only 'side effect' is an overall improvement in health. Regardless, what pharmaceutical agent can simultaneously treat the full scope of major killers: heart disease, hypertension, cancer, and diabetes, even Alzheimer's disease? Where in modern medicine is there an agent which successfully treats degenerative diseases of the major internal organs, even reversing these conditions? What possible medical therapy can obliterate pain and inflammation while also dramatically improving digestion and assimilation? The fact is with drug therapy it is the opposite, since all the potent antiinflammatory agents disrupt the digestive system, even categorically damaging it. They are, actually, so noxious, for instance non-steroidal antiinflammatory agents, that they routinely cause bleeding ulcers in the gut, which can prove fatal. Even aspirin does this, including the so-called baby type. Turmeric does the opposite, soothing the intestinal membranes and may even be used to heal ulcers, while stemming bleeding. In fact, because of its astringent powers it is an ideal natural medicine to administer for internal bleeding.

It is, then, an absolute cure for human disease: a vast range of them. Moreover, in this regard it achieves miracles for people on a daily basis: countless millions of them. Quietly and subtly, it heals the human body, cleansing all manner of corruption such as noxious toxin accumulations, diseased cells, and precancerous tissue as well as actual tumors. Incidentally, it cleanses the human lymphatic system in a most remarkable way, so the body can heal itself regardless of the affliction. Self-healing is the ultimate in therapeutic approaches. Thank God for wild and organic turmeric. They can precisely achieve this.

Is it not astounding? All this healing is occurring and a person can hardly even sense it. That is the miracle of nature, in fact, of the turmeric spice. While its inducing healing it is also stimulating digestive processes, boosting absorption and eliminating bloating as well as gas. Then, too, it acts on the senses, improving both hearing and vision, while regarding the eyes it seems to clear them, improving their appearance.

Now, with inflammation there can be no doubt about its powers, and these are highly sophisticated. Turmeric and its extracts act aggressively against inflammatory processes, easing pain, irritation, and swelling. For chronic pain it is one of the few natural drugs which achieves dependable results. While it achieves this, it reduces the dependancy on pharmaceutical agents, which may save great costs as well as lives.

The nervous system benefits, too, both in prevention and treatment. Certainly, there is prevention of neurodegeneration, including that seen in dementia and Alzheimer's disease. Regular intake may fully stall the development of diseases of neurodegeneration, keeping a person mentally fit well into old age. It also has actions in reversing brain damage, including the damage from stroke and trauma, while also aiding in the treatment of multiple sclerosis, ALS, and Parkinson's disease.

Then, too, the overall appearance of the human body is altered, often dramatically, as turmeric cleanses all internal systems: the bloodstream, lymph, and internal organs. Because of its astringent powers and antioxidant capacity it tones and preserves the skin, creating a youthfulness that no exotic cream, no high-end lotion, could ever achieve.

So, take advantage of it. The almighty creator produced its magnificence, making it a clear and obvious remedy. It is here for a specific purpose; it has that brilliant, bright color for a reason: so that it can be recognized for what it is. That is a beaming energy for all people's lives, enlivening, vitalizing, and invigorating them to the fullness of the extreme. This is through keeping the body as healthy as possible and also reversing, even purging, all pathology. Nothing could be more supreme than this.

So, again, take advantage of it. Use it in all its forms, as a food, spice, and whole food extract. The ideal extract is made from wild plants, while the top-quality root and spice are derived from both certified organic plants and the wild-growing type. If using commercial spice, be sure to use only non-irradiated sources. Yet, let us all strive for organic sources. This will drive the industry in the necessary direction for all in the future.

There are a number of recipes and remedies found in this book plus unique formulations, like numerous types of turmeric milk and also the pre-made emulsified spice in virgin, organic coconut oil. A raw, wild honey blended with wild turmeric, ginger, and cinnamon is available, which is delicious and health-giving. There is that unique supplement made as mycellized sublingual drops, with raw CO_2 extracted turmeric plus wild oregano and rosemary oils for aggressive and rapid absorption, along with potency of the highest degree. Consider also that ultra-power combination formula, complexing the wild turmeric with the organic, raw CO_2 hemp stalk extract, known as Canacurmin. As well, there is the golden/turmeric milk pre-mix, delicious to the extreme, which contains wild turmeric plus organic Ceylon cinnamon and ginger. A turmeric-ginger-cinnamon wild honey is also available. There is turmeric paste that can be made at home. Find other novel ways to incorporate it into your life. Through regular use life will be better and more productive. That's the wild turmeric guarantee.

Appendix A

Nutritional Supplements and Natural Formulas Mentioned in this Book

Wild turmeric sublingual drops with wild oregano, organic ginger extract, and wild rosemary (Turmeric-PLUS Mycellized Sublingual Drops)

Wild turmeric plus wild oregano and rosemary capsules (Turmeric-PLUS 500 mg gelcaps)

Wild turmeric powder plus ginger/cinnamon emulsion (CocaSpice)

Wild, edible daily use oregano oil (Oreganol P73)

Wild, raw chaga sublingual drops (Chag-o-Power drops)

Wild chaga-birch bark tea (ChagaBlack)

Total body purging agent (Total Body Purge)

Wild, raw dandelion leaf plus root extract (Dand-o-Max)

Wild, raw chaga capsules plus birch bark and wild oregano (ChagaMax capsules)

Whole food wild oregano crude herb plus *Rhus coriaria* (OregaMax capsules)

Oil of Black Seed (with fennel seed oil)

Black Seed-Plus capsules

Whole food vitamin complex (Purely-PAK)

Whole food, non-GMO vitamin E (Purely-E)

Whole food, non-GMO vitamin C complex (Purely-C)

Whole food, non-GMO vitamin B complex (Purely-B)

Wild rosemary essence (Essence of Wild Rosemary)

Wild oregano juice/essence (Juice of Wild Oreganol)

Edible, daily use wild rosemary oil (Rosemanol)

High-quality rose essence (Essence of Rose Blossoms)

High-quality neroli orange water (Essence of Orange Blossoms)

3x royal jelly with wild rosemary and sage (Royal Power)

Antiinflammatory enzyme complex with bromelain, turmeric, ginger, and papain (InflamEEZ)

CO_2 cannabis extract (Hempanol, regular and SuperStrength)

Freeze-dried black raspberry powder (RaspaMax)

Wild raspberry root and leaf syrup (RaspaSyrup)

Whole food digestive enzyme complex combined with spice concentrates (Gastronex)

Wild, raw multiple berries complex (Super-5-Berries)

Vegetarian (plant-source) probiotic supplement (HealthBAC)

Radiation-purging capsules made with bentonite, zeolite, and chlorella (Toxi-Purge)

HerbSorb spice mix

Whole food fatty salmon oil, rich in naturally occuring vitamins A and

D (PolarPower)

Cold-pressed Sesame (Sesame oil)

Neuroloft Essence, for healthy brain support

Cha's brand certified organic turmeric, ginger, and cinnamon

Oregulin sublingual drops, useful for blood sugar control and in addiction syndromes

Canacurmin Mycellized Sublingual Drops

Cancurmin high potency 500 mg gelcaps

North American Herb & Spice (NAHS) TurmaMilk Turmeric Milk and Food Mix

NAHS TurmaSpice High-Curcumin and High-Turmerone Wild Turmeric Powder

TurmaSpice Wild Oregano Honey, also by NAHS

To view these products or to order see: www.americanwildfoods.com. For a store near you that carries many of the high-quality products listed, here, see the store finder at www.oreganol.com.

Appendix B

Turmeric-based Supplements and Formulas Recommended in this Book

This is a summary of all the turmeric-based supplements, foods, and formulas specifically recommended in this book. The recommendations are based on exceptional quality and purity and also assurance that the products are lead- and chemical-free as well as devoid of all GMOs:

Turmeric-PLUS Mycellized Sublingual Drops (formerly Turmerol)

Turmeric-PLUS 500 mg gelcaps (formerly Turmerol)

Canacurmin Mycellized Sublingual Drops

Cancurmin high potency 500 mg gelcaps

CocaSpice

Cha's brand certified organic turmeric, ginger, and cinnamon

North American Herb & Spice (NAHS) TurmaMilk Turmeric Milk and Food Mix

NAHS TurmaSpice High-Curcumin and High-Turmerone Wild Turmeric Powder

TurmaSpice Wild Oregano Honey, also by NAHS

InflamEEZ capsules

To view these supplements and foods or to order see www.americanwildfoods.com

Bibliography

ScienceDaily.com. *More Dangerous Chemicals in Everyday Life: Now, Experts Warn Against Nanosilver.* Feb. 27, 2014. Science News.

ScienceDaily.com. *Toxic Nanoparticles Might be Entering Human Food Supply.* Aug. 22, 2013. Science News.

Adnyana, K., et al. 2014. Gastric ulcer healing effect of wild honey and its combination with turmeric rhizome on male Wistar rats. *J. Chinese Pharm.* Sci. 23:844.

Aggarwal, B.B., Kumar, A., and A.C. Bharti. 2003. Anticancer potential of curcumin: preclinical and clinical studies. *Anticancer Research.* 23:363.

Ahmed, T., Enam, S.A., Gilani, A.H., et al. 2010. Curcuminoids enhance memory in an amyloid-infused rat model of Alzheimer's disease. *Neruoscience.* 169:1296.

Ammon, H.P. and M.A. Wahl. Pharmacology of Curcuma longa. *Planta Medica.* 57:1-7.

Bamberger, M.E. and G.E. Landreth. 2002. Inflammation, apoptosis, and Alzheimer's disease. *Neuroscientist.* 8:276.

Chakravarty, A.K., Chatterjee, S.N., Yasmin, H., and T. Mazumder. 2009. Comparison of efficacy of turmeric and commercial curcumin in immunological functions and gene regulation. *Int. J. Pharm.* 5:333-345.

Chainani-Wu, N. 2003. Safety and antiinflammatory activity of curcumin: a component of turmeric (*Curcuma longa*). *Journal of Alternative and Complementary Medicine.* Feb 9:161.

Ammon, HPT and MA Wahl. 1991. Pharmacology of Curcuma longa. *Planta Medica.* 57:1-7.

De, R., Kundu,. P. Swamaker, S., et al. 2009. *Antimicrobial activity of curcumin against Helicobacter pylori isolates from India and during infections in mice*. In: Antimicrob Agents, Chemother Ch. 53, 1592-597.

Essential Herbs Duke, James., Ph.D.,

Funk, J. L. Efficacy and mechanism of action of turmeric supplements in the treatment of experimental arthritis. *Arthritis Rheum*. 2006 Nov; 54 (11) 3452.64.

Gupta, S.C., et al. 2012. Discovery of curcumin, a component of golden spice and its miraculous biological activities. *Clin. Exp. Pharmacol.* 39:283-299.

Hucklenbroich, J., et al. 2014. Aromatic-turmerone induces neural stem cell proliferation in vitro and in vivo. *Stem Cell Res. Ther.* 5:100.

Ingram, C. ____. *The Cause for Cancer Revealed*. Buffalo Grove, IL: Knowledge House Publishers.

Ingram, C. 2015. *The Lyme Disease Cure*. Buffalo Grove, IL: Knowledge House Publishers.

Ingram, C. 2016. *The Cannabis Cure*. Buffalo Grove, IL: Knowledge House Publishers.

Ingram, C. 2016. *The Cure is in the Cupboard*. Buffalo Grove, IL: Knowledge House Publishers.

Jurenka, J.S. 2009. Antiinflammatory properties of curcumin: a major constitutent of Curcuma longa: a review of preclinical and clinical research. *Altern. Med. Rev.* 14:141-153.

Kim, D.C., et al. 2005. Curcuma longa extract protects against gastric ulcers by blocking H2 histamine recetors. *Biol. Pharm. Bull.* 28:2220-2224.

Kudkarni and his group of the Department of Biotechnology, Sinhgad College of Engineering, Pune, India

Lee, Y. 2009. Activation of apoptotic protein in U937 cells by a component of turmeric oil. *BMB Rep.* 28:96.

Mishra, S. and K. Palanivelu. 2008. The effect of curcumin (turmeric) on Alzheimer's disease: an overview. *Am. Indian Acad. Neurol.* 11:13-19.

Monserrath-Orellan-Paucar, A., et al. 2013. Insights from zebrafish and mouse models on the activity and safety of ar-turmerone as a potential drug candidate for the treatment of epilepsy. *PLOS One.* 8:e81634.

Murakami, A., Furukawa, I., Miyamoto, S., Tanaka, T., and H. Ohigashi. 2012. Curcumin combined with turmerones, essential oil components of turmeric, abolishes inflammation-associated mouse colon carcinogenesis. *Biofactors,* Dec. 11.

Panahi, Y., Hosseini, M. S., Khalili, N., Naimi, E., Majeed, M., and Sahebkar, A. 2015. Antioxidant and antiinflammatory effects of curcuminoid-piperine combination in subjects with metabolic syndrome: a randomized, controlled trial and an updated meta-analysis. *Clinical Nutrition.* 34:1101-1108.

Sikha, A., Harini, A., and L. P. Hedge. 2014. Pharmacological activities of wild turmeric (Curcuma aromatica Salisb): a review. *J. Pharm. Phyto.* 3:1-4.

Sun, J., et al. 2008. Preventive effects of curcumin and dexamethasone on lung transplantation-associated lung injury in rats. *Cancer Lett.* 192:145.

Wojdylo, A., et al. 2007. Antioxidant activity and phenolic compounds in 32 selected herbs. *Food Chem.* 105:940-949.

Zhang, L., et al. 2006. Curcuminoids enhance amyloid beta uptake by macrophages of Alzheimer's disease patents. *J. Alzheimers Dis.* 10:1-7.

A. Vyas publishing in Current Pharmac Des., 2013. Here, it was found that 19:2047.